Centering Prayer and Rebirth in Christ
on the Tree of Life

ALSO FROM KESS FREY AND PORTAL BOOKS

Human Ground, Spiritual Ground
Paradise Lost and Found
A Reflection on Centering Prayer's Conceptual Background

Centering Prayer
and Rebirth in Christ
on the Tree of Life

THE PROCESS OF INNER TRANSFORMATION

Kess Frey

[PORTAL BOOKS]

2013
PORTAL BOOKS
An imprint of Anthroposophic Press/SteinerBooks
610 Main St., Great Barrington, MA
www.steinerbooks.org

Cover and book design: William Jens Jensen
Cover image: fractal image background by Mack7777 (shutterstock.com)
Tree of Life image by Kess Frey and William Jens Jensen

LIBRARY OF CONGRESS CATALOGING-IN-PUBLICATION DATA

Frey, Kessler.
  Centering prayer and rebirth in Christ on the tree of life : the process of inner transformation / Kess Frey.
     pages cm
  Includes bibliographical references.
  ISBN 978-1-938685-04-0 (pbk.) — ISBN 978-1-938685-05-7 (ebook)
  1. Spirituality. 2. Contemplation. 3. Prayer. 4. Cabala. 5. Tree of life. I. Title.
  BF1999.F725 2013
  248—dc23

                                            2013015371

Contents

This book is dedicated to the Christian contemplative tradition and all who study, practice and support it; and to the memories of Jim Gordon and John Dan Reib, who first introduced me to the Tree of Life and Qabalah many years ago.

Acknowledgments

I am grateful to Diane Frey, my sister, for her insights and writing about the Tree of Life, without which this book probably could not have been written; to the teaching and writing of Dr. Paul Foster Case and Rev. Dr. Ann Davies; to the work of Fr. Thomas Keating; to Fr. Carl J. Arico for his encouragement and support; and to William Jens Jensen for the cover and book design. Finally, I want to acknowledge my complete dependency on inner spiritual sources of inspiration, guidance and motivation in my writing and elsewhere.

FOREWORD

This book is both "old wine" and "new wine" in a "new wineskin." Following after his previous book, *Human Ground, Spiritual Ground*, in *Centering Prayer and Rebirth in Christ on the Tree of Life*, Kess Frey focuses on the process of inner transformation brought about, with our consent and cooperation, by the divine presence and action. To give a framework for this, Kess introduces a Christian, contemplative interpretation of the Qabalistic Tree of Life. This living allegorical Tree is said to predate the birth of Jesus and to have its earthly roots in ancient Hebrew Mysticism. In this book, Christ, the Word of the Father, stands in the center of creation's Universal Tree of Life, and in the individual soul's true heart as the divine indwelling.

The redeeming work of mystical Christianity—known by other names in other times, places, languages and traditions—has been available to every member of the human family from the beginning of the world. This is suggested in John's gospel where we read: ... *the Word was God ... All things came into being through him ... What has come into being in him was life, and the life was the light of all people* (John 1:1–4). Thus, the light of Christ has been present since the beginning of creation. The perspective of mystical Christianity being available to all humans from the beginning involves what might be called "Vertical Time," the eternal divine presence breaking through into horizontal or chronological time. These two dimensions of time are symbolized by the Cross, where the intersecting point of vertical and horizontal beams is the eternal present moment.

Kess Frey is part of a new generation of thinkers and meditators dealing with and pondering the wealth of Centering Prayer in relation to various spiritual traditions as, for example in this book, Jewish Mysticism and Christian Qabalah. Kess is steeped in his practice and knowledge of Centering Prayer and the Christian contemplative tradition, which are the foundation of his approach to the Tree of Life. He offers this book as a bridge between outer Christianity and mystical Christianity, and as a contribution to Centering Prayer's conceptual background. The purpose of Centering Prayer's conceptual background is to support the actual practice of the prayer and the process of purification, healing and renewal in the soul that's carried on in our partnership with Christ through fidelity to the practice and our ongoing consent to God's presence and action working in us.

Mining the gold in this book does take some work on the part of the reader and, I would add, especially a reader new to the Tree of Life. It's suggested that the book be read at least twice, once to get a clear idea of the Tree and again to more easily see how the Tree may be related to Centering Prayer's conceptual background and the process of inner transformation or "rebirth in Christ." When thus read slowly and thoughtfully, this book elevates the mind, offering a new vision of our evolving life in Christ and Christ in us. Making your own drawings of the Tree and its parts is a good way to get acquainted with it and make it your own.

As presented in this book, the Tree of Life offers a helpful way of visualizing the work God does in us on the spiritual journey. An interesting paradox of this work and the path of Centering Prayer is that we're seeking to become what we already are, and we don't get there by trying but by God's grace—yet we do need to make some efforts and find the time to pray the prayer and remain faithful to it day-by-day. If we'll do our part by saying "yes" to this process and our inner relationship with God, then God will do God's part.

Contemplative Outreach has a very rich and evolving vision of theological principles. Principle number ten states: "We identify with the Christian contemplative heritage in which Centering Prayer is rooted. We recognize this heritage as the common ground for Christian unity." Kess's book *Human Ground, Spiritual Ground* celebrates this principle. Following this principle is number eleven: "We affirm our solidarity with the contemplative dimension of other religions and sacred traditions." His book *Centering Prayer and Rebirth in Christ on the Tree of Life* manifests this principle.

With this in mind, Kess says he wants to embrace the Tree of Life for the Christian contemplative tradition, so we may use it as a theological tool for relating to God's presence and action in us. He notes that both the Tree of Life and Christian contemplation have roots in the mysticism of the Torah or Old Testament. That is, both have roots in human experiences of Vertical Time involving direct outer and inner contacts with the living Lord God and his representatives—such as his angels, priests and prophets. For Christians, the climax of what's foretold and hoped for in the Old Testament is, of course, the incarnation of God's Word in the person of Jesus Christ and the treasures we now have in the New Testament where Vertical Time breaks through into horizontal time.

I cheer Kess on and applaud this book for its words that reach out across the centuries to show the common bond that exists in the teaching of world religions without diminishing the specialness and uniqueness of him being a transforming Christian.

> *Fr. Carl J. Arico*
> *Founding Member of Contemplative Outreach*
> *Author of* A Taste of Silence
> *January 31, 2013*

PREFACE

The idea for this book came to me in spring 2008, as I was studying some introductory papers on the Tree of Life by my sister, Diane Frey. I was struck by the discovery that the Tree and its workings could be used as an insightful model for the mysterious inner process of our soul's purification, healing and rebirth in Christ. The additional revelation of the dark "invisible Sphere," and its potential correlation to the gift of contemplation and "the cloud of unknowing," further persuaded me.

What's presented here is my interpretation of the Tree of Life and attempt to adapt some of its Qabalistic teachings to the conceptual background of Centering Prayer. There are other interpretations and applications of the Tree I know little or nothing about. The central aim of this book is to adapt the Tree of Life to the purposes of Centering Prayer and Christian Mysticism, and in so doing to illumine and broaden Centering Prayer's conceptual background. Toward this end, some creative liberties have been taken, especially regarding the dark, invisible Sphere, Daath, to which I've added the contemplative reference, "the Cloud."

This book breaks new ground for Centering Prayer's conceptual background. Building on what's already established, it offers a model of Christian transformation that's rooted in the ancient history of the Judeo-Christian Tradition; that is, in the "Secret Wisdom of Israel" and the Qabalistic Tree of Life which were, I believe, known to the Rabbi Jesus. The Tree of Life, representing the emanations and activities of the divine consciousness within the divine consciousness, is a dynamic map and symbol of both universal creation and the individual soul. As such, it offers a unique view of the hidden processes of creation's ongoing evolution and our spiritual growth—as we'll see in these pages.

This book is a Christian, contemplative interpretation of the Qabalistic Tree of Life. It's Christian in that Christ, the eternal Son and Word of God, is the living centerpiece of the Tree. The book's scope is contemplative in that it touches upon conceptual and non-conceptual, concentrative and receptive forms of meditation and contemplation.

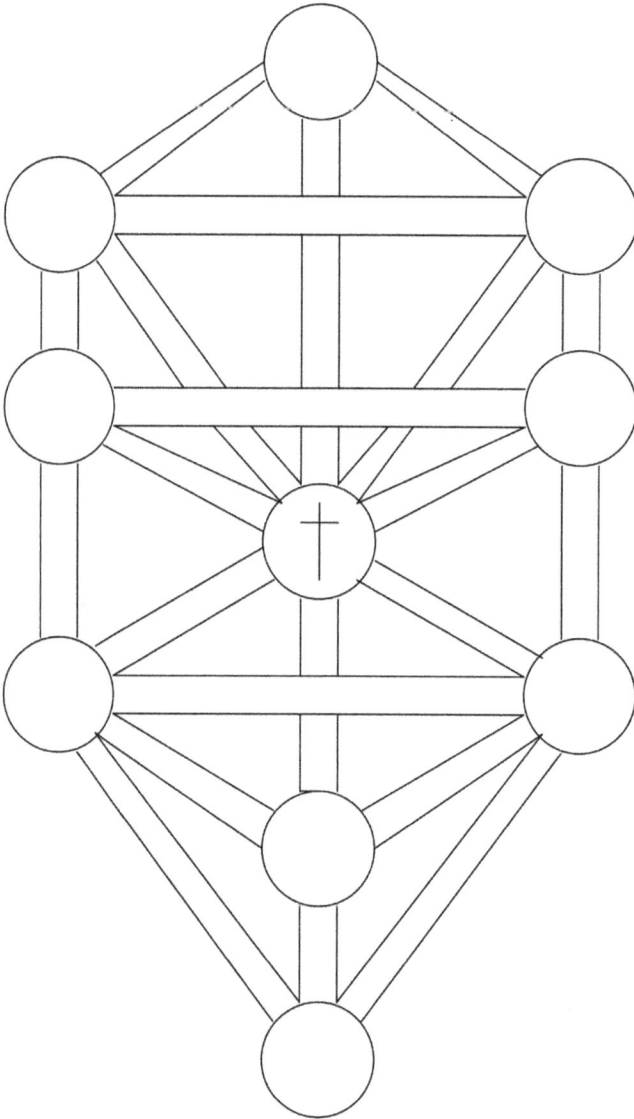

Basic Tree of Life Pattern

INTRODUCTION

I

This book is written in continuation of a previous work, *Human Ground, Spiritual Ground: Paradise Lost and Found*, which is a detailed reflection on the conceptual background of Centering Prayer as developed by Thomas Keating. While the prior book focuses primarily on the parameters of the human condition, our basic instinctual needs and the false-self system, this present work concerns the inner process of our transformation from false self to true self or rebirth in Christ. The Qabalistic Tree of Life is used here as a model for visualizing this process and our contemplative journey into God. These two books may be read independently or together as a complimentary set. Before discussing the Tree of Life in detail, I want to say a few things about Centering Prayer, its background and how these may relate to the Tree of Life:

Centering Prayer is a contemporary method of Christian practice aimed at opening us to the gift of contemplation, which is the gift of God's presence and action in us and in our life. We might call it "entry level contemplation," since it's a way of accessing this simple yet mysterious gift—which is not so much something we do as it's something God does in us, with our willing consent and cooperation. Centering Prayer, as taught by Contemplative Outreach, Ltd., originated in the mid-1970s at St. Joseph's Abbey in Spencer, Massachusetts.[1] Frs. Thomas Keating, William Meninger and Basil Pennington were its principal architects. The Christian contemplative tradition in general and the anonymously written fourteenth-century spiritual classic, *The Cloud of Unknowing*, in particular, are two of Centering Prayer's primary sources of inspiration.

An important scriptural source for Centering Prayer is Matthew 6:6, where Jesus gives the wisdom teaching: "When you pray, go into your inner room, close the door and pray to your Father in secret; and your Father who sees in secret will reward you." This concise wisdom teaching from Jesus is an invitation to the contemplative journey. As Thomas Keating has explained,[2] the "inner room," "private room" or "closet" (as some translations have it) is the spiritual level of our being, our soul's private inner space of heart and mind. "Closing" or "bolting" the door has to do with disengaging from all external and internal perceptions, distractions and preoccupations ("thoughts"), especially our own self-talk, so our awareness may receptively enter and effortlessly rest in the simplicity of God's immediate present moment. As Thomas Keating has said regarding the present moment, "You can't get to the bottom of it." This is a very important point for receptive contemplative practice.

Praying to our "Father in secret" is not merely praying in secret from others but in secret from our conscious self (false self) as well. In the context of Centering Prayer, "prayer in secret" is prayer in silence and prayer in the unconscious, which is where the real action and work of contemplative prayer happens. Jesus is hinting at this when he mentions our "Father who sees in secret." "The Unconscious" is a modern psychological term for that in us which exists "in secret" because it's outside our conscious awareness. Hence, real "prayer in secret" is secret from the person who does the praying. So, Centering Prayer, "prayer in secret" in our "inner room," is a prayer that's largely hidden from surface awareness in the unconscious depths of our soul. This is where God, the "Father who sees in secret," works in us, to give us the "reward" Jesus mentions.

What is this "reward?" It's not some prize, power or possession God gives us but something incomparably more wonderful. The "reward" is: we *become* the reward. That is, we are purified, healed and eventually reborn into Christ. An essential part of this process is what Thomas Keating calls the "unloading of the unconscious." The reward we receive gradually becomes transformation into our true self. This reward is infinitely greater than anything God could give us without changing us into the blossoming fullness of our holy inheritance as children of God created in the divine image. When "the Father who sees in secret" rewards us, what's happening in our unconscious manifests up into consciousness as we experience in daily life the fruits of Centering Prayer and our evolving life in Christ. The hidden process underlying our gradual rebirth into this marvelous reward or gift is a central focus of this book.

II

What opposes our spiritual growth and needs to be changed in us has been described by Thomas Keating in his conceptual background for Centering Prayer[3]; and, following from Thomas Keating's teaching, this has also been discussed in *Human Ground, Spiritual Ground*. To briefly summarize these ideas, we may note that human life happens within the context of four basic existential parameters or "fruits of the fall," to which we are all subject. These are 1) death/change (impermanence), 2) sex/desire (need and want), 3) good/evil choices (morality and free will), and 4) our innate existential aloneness/incompleteness apart from God (the dualistic ego-consciousness of our separate-self identity or false self). Within the framework of these four existential parameters, we are all born with certain basic instinctual needs that must be met to some minimal degree if we're to survive and experience health, growth and wellbeing in life.

Our basic instinctual needs may be identified as: security/survival/safety; sensation / pleasure; affection/esteem/approval; power/control; and intimacy / belonging. We are both human beings and spiritual beings. Hence, our basic instinctual needs take expression on all levels of our soul and life: physical, vital, emotional, mental, psychic, social and spiritual. Our soul is a multidimensional energy field capable of functioning on all levels of created reality. That is, our soul has roots in both earth and heaven, i.e., human ground and spiritual ground. Spiritual growth involves enrichment of our soul's energy field. The Tree of Life, as described in this book, is a map of this energy field—and more, as we shall see.

What opposes our human and spiritual growth has been called our "false self" or "false-self system." The core of the false self is our childish egocentric sense of absolute separate-self identity. Its motivational operating system is a unique set of emotional programs for happiness that are pathological distortions and exaggerations of our legitimate instinctual needs. These happiness programs are actually, as Thomas Keating has said, "programs for human misery." Another key aspect of the false self is over-identification with cultural conditioning and various groups to which we belong, either by fate or by choice.

The false-self system and its functioning tend to be unconscious in most of us most of the time. When the false self's happiness programs are frustrated or gratified, we tend to experience various over-reactive afflictive emotions that are liable to dominate consciousness and our behavior. Some typical examples of these are: pride, grief, fear, anger, ego-inflation or deflation, jealousy, greed, lust and apathy. These are outer, conscious symptoms of an inner disease. Over-compensation in any direction and emotional over-reactivity are telltale hallmarks of the false self. These are its basic, general symptoms.

Thomas Keating's expose of the false self in all of us is an insight of tremendous value and significance for the spiritual growth of sincere Christians seeking intimacy with God and rebirth in Christ, or for anyone seeking human health, freedom and spiritual growth. The false self, which opposes our human and spiritual growth, is an inevitable consequence of being born human. It tends to be a mixture of positive and negative qualities and has both gross and subtle manifestations. Its grosser manifestations become obvious, once we acknowledge the false self's reality and begin to look for its expressions or symptoms in us. On the other hand, the false self's subtler manifestations are somewhat more challenging to nuance, once we've begun to eliminate its grosser expressions on the obvious conscious level. This is because the false self's subtler manifestations tend to invade our better intentions and healthier activities on hidden motivational levels. Here, we enter the tricky arena of conflicting conscious and unconscious agendas, our human ego's self-image, and the subtle good/evil struggle of pure motivations versus mixed motivations.

This is tricky and challenging because the human mind is capable of seemingly endless self-deceptions and masquerades, especially when mixed motivations and hidden agendas of the false self are involved. Once our conscious surface-act is seemingly in order, uncovering the false self's subtler manifestations calls for carefully noticing the delicate differences between too much, not enough and the right amount regarding whatever we may need, do or desire, e.g., food, money, safety, pleasure, esteem, power, success or personal freedom. Too much and not enough are of the false self, and the right, healthy amount is of the true self. The right amount is always in harmony with true conscience (as opposed to false conscience) and gives us feelings of inner peace, contentment and wellbeing. Too little or too much, on the other hand, tend to leave us feeling restless, incomplete and dissatisfied, even when we get what we want and its initial enjoyment fades away.

How we end up feeling, as a result of what we do or don't do, is one way to nuance the subtle movements of false self and true self in us. We are dealing here with the conscious surface effects of an interior process whose workings are hidden in the unconscious. Being subject to divisions between consciousness and the unconscious is a basic limitation inherent to human nature and our evolving physical-brain consciousness.[4] Since the inner core and roots of the false-self system are unconscious, we may have no direct or immediate access to them on the conscious level. Thus, we cannot change the false self merely by an act of conscious will, though we may sorely want to; and this is why we need divine help on the inside from "the Father who sees in secret," to complete the job of transformation into our true self. We cannot do it on our own, as the false self. This is a key point regarding the inner processes of our purification, healing and rebirth in Christ.

III

The inner work of Centering Prayer is the work God does in our unconscious. This work aims at removing the unconscious causes of our conscious false-self symptoms. It aims at eliminating the obstacles in us that prevent us from fully living the gospel values in daily life. Our real obstacles are the hidden unconscious ones that block us from freely accessing our true self in spiritual ground, and from growing into union with Christ in our soul.

Christ's apostle, Peter, writes: "Like living stones, let yourselves be built into a spiritual house" (1 Peter 2:5, *New American Bible*). This expresses well what the agenda of Centering Prayer is all about. It's not we who do the building here but the divine presence and action working in us, given our willing consent and cooperation. This "building" is nothing less than a reconstruction of the unconscious patterns and motivations of our human personality and consciousness in accordance with the inner light of divine love, truth and freedom. We're to be "built into a spiritual house" both individually and collectively, our collective spiritual identity being our mystical life in Christ or the "New Jerusalem."

In the New Jerusalem or Mystical Body of Christ, there is a confluence of individual identities in the great "I Am" of God's Word and only Son within all of us. In this heavenly place of unity in Christ's love, individual souls are differentiated without being isolated. This confluence of unique identities in Christ is similar to the confluence and relationships of Father, Son and Holy Spirit we may imagine in the Trinity.

Jesus speaks of these things in the Last Supper Discourses where he says: "On that day you will realize that I am in my Father and you are in me and I in you" (John 14:20). And: "I will ask the Father, and he will give you another Advocate to be with you always, the Spirit of truth, which the world cannot accept, because it neither sees nor knows it. But you know it, because it remains with you, and will be in you" (John 14:16–17.) Thus, what the Father does "in secret" is also done by the Son and the Holy Spirit, owing to the confluence of their identities in the oneness of the Godhead. Awakening, by God's grace, to our life in Christ and Christ in us is a fundamental aim of contemplative prayer and Christian mysticism.

IV

In Christian Tradition, the two general categories for contemplative prayer are called "kataphatic" (with images) and "apophatic" (without images). Centering Prayer is a method for accessing the gift of apophatic contemplation, which is totally receptive and non-conceptual. As Thomas Keating has explained, apophatic contemplation is "pure contemplation," the deepest contemplation that leads to union with God beyond thoughts, feelings, words, images and particular experiences.[5] Kataphatic contemplation, on the other hand, uses the imagination and is more concentrative than receptive. Kataphatic contemplation is something that we do, for example, in visualizing images or focusing on objects of worship, bible texts, sacred ritual, theological concepts or specific prayers—like the Lord's Prayer. Apophatic contemplation, on the other hand, is something that God does in us.

Prayer with images (kataphatic contemplation) is preparation for the deeper non-conceptual prayer beyond images (apophatic contemplation) where God—as invisible Father, Son and Holy Spirit—becomes most fully active in our soul. It's important to realize that these two types of spiritual practice are mutually complementary. That is, taken together, kataphatic and apophatic contemplation round out our prayer life into an integrated whole. They prepare our soul's inner ground for each other's deepening in us as we grow in our prayer life.

The Qabalistic Tree of Life, as a composite diagram representing each individual soul and the ten universal Spheres of emanation and activity of the divine consciousness, is a complex image for kataphatic contemplation. Given this fact, one may well ask: what is the connection between apophatic Centering Prayer and the kataphatic Tree of Life master-symbol? In addition to offering an enlightening window on our soul's inner structure and workings—e.g., the mysterious processes of our inner purification, healing and spiritual awakening—the Tree of Life holds a vital entry point for the gift of apophatic contemplation.

What is this entry point? Besides and within the ten Spheres of emanation and activity on the Tree of Life, there is also an invisible dark Sphere, called "Daath," that may not be accurately imagined or conceived by the intellect, an "apophatic Sphere."[6] This sphere is associated with "crossing the abyss" of unconsciousness and may be identified with the "cloud of unknowing" from the anonymous four-teenth-century spiritual classic mentioned earlier. The Tree of Life's enigmatic dark invisible Sphere is where kataphatic spiritual practices end and evolve into receptive, apophatic processes of deep contemplation where we may "allow" ourselves "to be built into a spiritual house." The Qabalistic Tree of Life may not be fully embraced or known without crossing the non-conceptual abyss of Daath, its hidden invisible Sphere. This correlates to the need of receiving the gift of apophatic contemplation in order to complete our spiritual journey from false-self consciousness into rebirth in Christ and its divine transforming union.

V

For readers new to the Tree of Life, an easy way to develop a sense of the Tree is to do some drawings of it while studying it: You may copy some of the diagrams in this book as well as create your own. It seems the physical act of drawing the Tree, coloring and labeling its parts helps to impress it in the mind. By repeatedly visualizing the Tree of Life and its aspects, one gradually internalizes it and develops an intuitive working knowledge of the Tree. When studied and meditated upon, the Tree, together with its symbolic connections and implications, may yield many helpful fruits of inspiration and insight.

PART ONE: THE TREE OF LIFE

MEETING THE TREE

The Qabalistic Tree of Life presents what is, for me, an astonishing map of created reality's energy field and the soul's transformation into spiritual awakening. Taken as a whole and meditated upon, the Tree-of-Life map has the capacity to greatly enlarge our vision and understanding of the soul's inner world. This map, reportedly derived from the "Secret Wisdom of Israel," describes God's ongoing creation of the Universe and of each individual soul according to the pattern of the Tree's visible image, which I see as a very good and complete representation of the "divine image" mentioned in Genesis 1:26–27. According to B.O.T.A. teaching,[1] the Qabalah, which includes the Tree of Life, was given to humanity by the angels over six thousand years ago as a way of returning to God.

I first heard of the Tree of Life in 1966, when a college friend began studying Qabalah privately with his English teacher, John Dan Reib, at Pasadena City College in Southern California. He introduced me to John Dan and through occasional meetings and conversations I began to learn a little about the Tree. My main interests at that time were Depth Psychology, Christian Mysticism and Eastern Philosophy, so, though I was curious and interested in the Tree, I had little time to devote to its study. I was then also quite occupied as a full-time student at the University of California, Irvine. I did, however, manage to read one book recommended by my friend and John Dan Reib, *The Mystical Qabalah* by Dion Fortune—a classic in its field. Ms. Fortune's book was fascinating but overwhelmingly complex for me; yet it did leave me with a general idea of the Tree of Life and its rich symbolism.

My friendship and occasional meetings with John Dan continued, and over the years I read a few works concerning Qabalah and the Tree of Life. Another valuable source of information on the Tree has been my sister, Diane Frey, who studied for some years with Dr. Ann Davies at the B.O.T.A., beginning in the early 1970s. In the past ten or so years, I have studied and reflected on published books and audio CDs from the B.O.T.A. concerning the Tree of Life and its traditions. This outer input, along with a number of intuitive inner experiences, has increased my limited understanding of Qabalah and the Tree of Life. Also, Diane has written some introductory papers on the Tree and these, along with numerous conversations, have greatly enriched and aided my understanding and appreciation of Qabalah. Since one definition of Qabalah is "revealed teaching," all that we discover intuitively is, in a sense, Qabalistic.

My initial desire to combine the Tree of Life with Centering Prayer came from discovering that the Tree offers some clear imagery for describing the soul's invisible transformation from false self to true self. I see the Tree as containing an insightful map of the dynamics of what Thomas Keating has called "divine therapy" and "inner resurrection." As such, I feel this view of the Tree may helpfully contribute to the conceptual background of Centering Prayer. Also, I've learned that the Tree of Life gives a detailed, step-by-step view of how God is creating the Universe and sustaining each individual soul within it. The Tree is a living template for the inner correspondence and identity of God and the soul, Macrocosm and microcosm, the divine image in humans and humans created in the divine image. This comprehensive spiritual map articulates the soul's inner world, has many applications, and may usefully complement other maps of the spiritual journey.

The challenge for me here is to present my particular interpretation of this map to readers unfamiliar with the Tree of Life in a way that is at once clear, understandable and in service to this book's intentions. Owing to this and my very limited knowledge of Qabalah and the Tree, I'll try to keep things as simple as possible by focusing on key points, necessary details and basic essentials. Consequently, much more that could be said will have to be left unsaid.

In what follows, I'll try to make the above points regarding false-self/true-self, transformation, Universal Creation, Macrocosm/microcosm and the divine image in our soul clear. In order to do so, I'll need to give an outline description of the Tree of Life and to introduce some traditional Qabalistic terminology—which comes from the original Hebrew words for the dynamic energy-centers or Spheres, called *Sephira* (sing.) and *Sephiroth* (pl.), on the Tree. I'll try to keep new terminology to a minimum. Another challenge will be to both integrate and separate newer Christian concepts, like the Holy Trinity, and older Qabalistic concepts, like the Three Triads of Sephiroth on the Tree that precede and feed into the final tenth Sephira of outer physical manifestation.

Traditional Christian and Qabalistic concepts represent two different maps of the same invisible processes and spiritual terrain. Comparing different visible maps of the one universal spiritual territory and its mysterious processes may help us gain a fuller, clearer understanding of what that invisible reality is actually like. Assuming they're accurate representations, comparing different spiritual maps may be analogous to viewing a mountain from different sides of its base, i.e., North, South, East and West. In doing so, we may learn more about the total mountain and the different paths to its summit, i.e., our spiritual goal.

In comparing spiritual maps and forming concepts about the invisible spiritual world, there's bound to be a certain amount of vagueness, not only among different maps but within specific individual maps as well. This holds true even when these ideas are inspired by direct personal experiences of the spiritual world's awesome Mystery. Our maps are, after all, human creations and vagueness is inevitable since we are forming mentally visible concepts and diagrams to represent an inner reality that generally transcends and is invisible to our mental gaze. Consequently, the same fundamental spiritual ideas may be conceived of differently even within the same spiritual tradition. For example, there are differences in how Christians may describe the Holy Trinity and its functioning, e.g., as being exclusively masculine, as in Western Christianity, or with the Holy Spirit being feminine, as in Orthodox Christianity. As we shall see, the view of the Holy Spirit as feminine is much closer to Qabalistic concepts, which emphasize masculine-feminine polarities and energy-flow within and among the Sephiroth and throughout the Tree of Life.

Looking at the famous prologue to St. John's Gospel (John 1:1-18), we may say, in terms of the Holy Trinity, that God, the Father, intends and conceives the plan for creation; and that God, the Son or Word, carries this plan out. In Qabalah, the same creation is taking place, but the description of the process of creation is more detailed and nuanced, in terms of the roles or functions of specific Sephira on the Tree of Life. Qabalah identifies four progressive Worlds or levels of creation through which the process works its way down the Tree into outer physical manifestation. This process of progressive unfolding begins with God, at the top of the Tree, and then follows a set pattern down through the Sephiroth in various inner realms to finally culminate in the tenth Sephira, corresponding to the fourth World or outer realm of manifestation at the bottom of the Tree.

So, there are obvious differences in how Qabalah and traditional Christian theology describe God's creation of the heavens, underworld, Earth and Universe. However, in spite of seeming differences, there are some important connections between Qabalah and Christianity, since Jesus was, after all, of the Hebrew Tradition and was probably well acquainted with the "Secret Wisdom of Israel." According to B.O.T.A. teaching, Jesus was the greatest of all Qabalistic masters.

The idea of "secret wisdom" or "secret teachings" has been around for a long time and may be found in all of the world's religious and spiritual traditions, e.g., yogis in Hinduism, Vajrayana Buddhism, mystics and contemplatives in Christianity, Qabalists in Judaism and Sufis in Islam. The idea of outer teachings for the general followers of a tradition versus inner teachings for those who are more mature, educated or advanced has also been referred to as the exoteric (outer) versus the esoteric (inner) ways of understanding and practicing a given religion or spiritual path. The esoteric ways are identified as being for those who are more fully prepared, committed and who seek direct, personal and intimate experiential relationship with their tradition and the living God. Such an inner or esoteric path tends to be more demanding than the normal outer ways of religious belief and practice.

I've noticed a few places in the gospels where Jesus appears to be hinting at or implying an inner or esoteric level of teaching. The first of these occurs in Matthew 13:10–12 where his disciples ask him, "Why do you speak to them in parables?" Jesus replies, "The mystery of the kingdom of heaven has been granted to you. But to those outside everything comes in parables." Outer and inner teachings are implied here.

This is not to minimize the importance of the parables, which, as Thomas Keating and others have stressed, constitute a major part of the authentic teaching of Jesus that's available to us.[2] The point here is that this question to Jesus from his close disciples, together with the master's answer, suggests another, more directly experiential level of his teaching that the disciples had access to but not the general public whom he taught with parables. Unfortunately, beyond what we find in Matthew 6:6, scripture does not appear to tell us much more about the inner level of teaching and practice that prompted the disciples' question to Jesus regarding his use of parables.

A second place where Jesus clearly suggests an inner level of teaching in the Hebrew Tradition may be found in Matthew 23:13–14 where Jesus rebukes the religious teachers of his day. He says to them, "Woe to you Scribes and Pharisees, you hypocrites. You lock the kingdom of heaven before human beings. You do not enter yourselves, nor do you allow entrance to those trying to enter."

And again, in Luke 11:52, Jesus says, "Woe to you, scholars of the law! You have taken away the keys of knowledge. You yourselves did not enter and you stopped those trying to enter." Apparently, the scribes, Pharisees and scholars of the law had betrayed their spiritual responsibility to the people they served in favor of false-self agendas. These understandably harsh words from Jesus tell us that the Hebrew scribes, Pharisees and scholars of the law possessed or had access to the inner teaching and key knowledge of how to enter God's inner presence *before* he, Jesus, appeared on the scene. What else could these inner teachings be but the "Secret Wisdom of Israel," the Qabalah, Tree of Life and their spiritual practices?

The visible Tree of Life glyph is a mirror-reflection of what's invisible manifested in the visible. It's a living master symbol of the inner worlds and outer creation alive and happening within the divine consciousness of non-created Reality (God). The ten visible Spheres or Sephiroth on the Tree of Life are, among other things, the dwelling places of all kinds of higher, intermediate and lower visible and invisible beings. These various conscious nonphysical entities include discarnate souls and range from mighty archangels and perfected spiritual masters in the highest sacred realms to all the way down the Tree where dark demons, animal spirits, and elementary entities inhabit its lower levels. We humans are among the conscious beings living in the Tree's all-inclusive energy field.

The relatively newer Christian ideas and spiritual maps are also revealed (Qabalistic) teachings inspired by Christ and the Holy Spirit. They were initially created on Earth by oral traditions, the gospel and other New Testament writers, and fathers and mothers of the Church during the first centuries of Christianity; and have been further elaborated down to the present by various saints, mystics, artists and theologians of the Church. In Christian art, music, literature and theology, we have a marvelous wealth of spiritual imagery and inspiration that speaks to our deep inner self and longing for closeness to God.

I believe Qabalah and the Tree of Life have something real, vital and enriching to offer our Christian maps of the inner worlds and spiritual journey. The Tree is a universal master symbol with many possible applications. For interested individuals, the model of the soul's inner working accessible on the Tree significantly enlarges our view and may helpfully complement various Christian contemplative maps, such as those created by Teresa of Avila, John of the Cross and Thomas Keating.[3] This book is intended to demonstrate this.

An important but not widely known book linking Christian spirituality with the Tree of Life and Qabalah is *Meditations on the Tarot: A Journey into Christian Hermeticism*. I first became aware of this book in July 1989, through Fr. Theophane Boyd of Saint Benedict's Monastery in Snowmass, Colorado, where I was on private retreat. This highly unusual, monumental work was written anonymously and published posthumously at the wishes of its author, a French cleric who was obviously a well-educated, dedicated Christian with a keen recognition and awareness of how Western Hermeticism (of which Qabalah and the Tree of Life are integral parts) can illuminate and enrich Christian spirituality. Originally published in English in 1985, the 2002 edition of *Meditations on the Tarot* features an afterword by Cardinal Hans Urs von Balthasar, "widely considered one of the greatest Catholic theologians of the twentieth century" and "nominated by Pope John Paul II."

Owing to this book's cover title, and to negative cultural conditioning, prejudice and ignorance regarding what the Tarot actually is, as a concentrative tool for transforming the human psyche and opening to spiritual awakening, this book would likely be misjudged, unappreciated and rejected at apparent face value by many contemporary Christians. However, this has not been the case for all Christians. Regarding *Meditations on the Tarot*, Thomas Keating is quoted on the back cover as saying, "This book, in my view, is the greatest contribution to date toward the rediscovery and renewal of the Christian contemplative tradition of the Fathers of the Church and the High Middle Ages." Basil Pennington commented, "It is without doubt the most extraordinary work I have ever read. It has tremendous spiritual depth and insight." And Father Bede Griffiths: "It is simply astonishing. I have never read such a comprehensive account of the 'perennial philosophy.'...There is hardly a line without some profound significance.... To me it is the last word in wisdom."

I believe these enthusiastic endorsements from three well-known and highly respected Christian contemplatives were made in the mid-1980s. I've included them here to help support my claim that Qabalah and the Tree of Life have much of value to contribute to Christian maps of the spiritual journey, especially in its practical, mystical and contemplative aspects (both kataphatic and apophatic as explained earlier). At this point, one may wonder, what is the relationship between Tarot, Qabalah and the Tree of Life?

The important connection between Tarot and the Tree of Life, which will not be discussed in any detail here, is as follows: There are twenty-two energy paths or channels on the Tree of Life linking the various Sephiroth and allowing them to interact with one another. In ancient Hebrew Qabalah, these twenty-two energy paths are each associated with one of the twenty-two letters of the Hebrew alphabet, which, like Greek letters, are also numbers. As the divine energy of creation moves down the Tree of Life, it changes its modes of expression. These specific energy-changes are characterized by the twenty-two Hebrew letters, which are associated with the corresponding twenty-two energy paths linking the ten Sephiroth.

Paul Foster Case was a long-time student of Tarot. When he founded Builders of the Adytum (Inner Temple), he was inspired by inner vision to place the twenty-two Major Arcana or Keys of the Tarot, in their numerical sequence (0 to 21), on the corresponding twenty-two energy paths linking the ten Sephiroth from top to bottom on the Tree of Life. These archetypal symbols reveal the qualities and workings of the energies that flow along the twenty-two paths, as do the Hebrew letters, which Dr. Case also included. In this we have the important connection between the twenty-two Tarot Keys (which may be used for kataphatic visualization and meditation) and the Tree of Life.

According to B.O.T.A. teaching, this "Secret Wisdom" of Qabalah and the Tree of Life, which requires a lot of study and meditation, was the inner teaching or key to spiritual knowledge in the Hebrew Tradition at the time of Jesus. This esoteric Judaism was, allegedly, the actual religion *of* Jesus, i.e., the religion Jesus was trained in and practiced (perhaps during the eighteen years of his life not accounted for in the New Testament). Some have suggested Jesus acquired this "Secret Wisdom of Israel" by studying with the Essene Brotherhood at their Dead Sea Community, which was not too distant from where he lived.[4] Unproven as this is by any physical archaeological evidence, it's certainly a possibility. In any case, Jesus must have undergone some study and training in order to become a rabbi. No doubt, the living essence of what Jesus taught was revealed to him (in true Qabalistic fashion) directly by God the Father.

Jesus brought the new Christian revelation of God's precious love into the world, manifesting the highest value of our soul's preciousness and fulfillment. This greatest of spiritual events in human history initiated the pivotal turning point in the evolution of human consciousness toward divine consciousness as the eternal Word of God became fully embodied and manifested in the fragile flesh of human ground.

Since that time, the "divine image," for Christians, has become what St. Paul referred to as "Christ in us, the hope of glory" (Col. 1:27). In Christian Qabalah, Christ is the active, dynamic centerpiece on the Tree of Life, the redeemer and one Son of God dwelling in the heart and true center of each soul.

2

THE DIVINE IMAGE

Then God said, "Let us make humankind in our image, according to our likeness; and let them have dominion over the fish of the sea." So God created humankind in his image, in the image of God he created them; male and female he created them (Gen. 1:26–27)

The divine image in us is the priceless jewel of our soul. It is the pattern of our inner growth and awakening to life in Christ, as conscious members of Christ's Mystical Body. The divine image in us is our greatest treasure. It's the imprint of what God intends us to uniquely become as our true self in human ground and spiritual ground. So what is our creation in the form of this divine image? The Tree of Life offers some answers to this question.

I've noticed at least two paradoxes in the above, well-known quote from Genesis. The first of these is the paradox of the divine image itself: If God is non-created Reality, how can non-created Reality have an image when all images exist within created reality? A short answer to this paradox is that the divine image is formed in creation by God's divine plan and by the practical working structure for implementing that plan. In Qabalah, the practical working structure for manifesting God's plan is the Tree of Life. The divine image is, then, a visible mirror-reflection in created reality of the invisible non-created God's intention to create. Created reality is God's self-expression which reveals something of God according to our capacity to perceive. Further discussion of God's divine image will follow below.

A second seeming paradox in the above quote from Genesis is: If God is one, to whom is God speaking when he says, "Let us make humankind in our image, according to our likeness?" This is the paradox of the One and the Two: How can the One also be Two? An answer to this question, and others, may also be found on the Tree of Life, which is a map of consciousness including all levels of creation. The One and the Two of God exist on different levels of creation within the One; this will be explained in more detail below as we describe the Tree of Life and its workings.

Creation requires two on all levels. That is, it requires two complementary separate poles, positive and negative, and the movement of energy back and forth between them. So in order for creation to happen, the one indivisible God has to divide into the Original Two within the One. The One is the first Sephira on the Tree of Life and the Two are the second and third Sephiroth. Dividing into the Two is the birth of the divine Masculine and Feminine Principles within the One. These primordial Two are known in Qabalah as Divine Cosmic Father and Divine Cosmic Mother. It is these two primordial emanations of the One God that are the "us" speaking to each other within the One, and who say, "Let us make humankind in our image, according to our likeness." The Divine Cosmic Father and Mother are the archetypal male and female expressions of the divine nature, present and manifested throughout the Tree of Life in all its Sephiroth, throughout creation and in every human being. This is fundamental.

We are created in the divine image on all levels, physically in terms of our "clothes of skin" (Gen. 3:21)—i.e., our outer male and female physical bodies—and spiritually in terms of the inner structure and functioning of our soul, which is a microcosmic replica of the universal Tree of Life. What God does in created reality is done through God's emanations, called "Sephiroth," on the Tree of Life, both in us and in the great wide Universe of physical and nonphysical creation. Returning to the paradox of the divine image: non-created Reality's image is God's divine intention and plan for creation as manifested through the universal Tree of Life and in each of us. In order to complete the divine image in us, we need to become it by, with God's help, fully manifesting its divine potential in our soul.

So, the divine intention (motivation) and design of creation itself (that design being the Tree of Life) *are* the divine image. Since created reality is God's self-expression, creation is the manifested mirror-reflection of what, in itself, can have no image; that is, non-created Reality. Here we have the divine paradox of what's invisible and beyond creation becoming visible in creation: that is, becoming visible to us, in us and through us. This is accomplished via the creative work and play God is manifesting by giving us free will and in ultimately fulfilling the divine plan for creation in us and through us. As microcosms of the Macrocosm, we *are* the Tree of Life and divine image.

Created reality is God's self-expression, and God's divine plan for created reality is to manifest perfection (God's image and likeness) as ideal Beauty (God's only begotten Son) on all levels of creation. This plan is a work in progress and we are all invited to join in this Great Work or *Magnum Opus*. God's plan for creation and the practical means for manifesting it pre-exist in the divine consciousness as a point of intention in non-created Reality that gives birth to the Tree of Life. This plan is a mirror-reflection of non-created Reality that God intends to express in created reality, so that all souls may behold its glory and become conscious living images of its self-reflection, i.e., Sons and Daughters of God. So, the divine image is God's plan for creation, the means for manifesting it and the completion of its work both in us and throughout the Universe. God's "likeness" consists in the attitudes and qualities that express the divine nature. God's divine plan is clearly a *magnum opus* in progress, so far as human ground, our souls and the physical Universe are concerned.

We cannot reduce or limit the divine image to any picture or humanly conceived idea, though we may represent it by images and ideas such as those of the Tree of Life and Holy Trinity. Interpreting God's divine plan and the means for creation's manifestation and perfection as being the divine image does not reduce the non-created God to a created thing. It simply reveals the divine plan for creation to be God's intention for full self-expression in created reality, which is where all desires and images must manifest or attempt to manifest. Whenever creative activity leads to true self-expression, what is produced is always a mirror-reflection of whoever creates it. Hence, this ideal plan and God's way of manifesting it through Christ, God's Son, on the Tree *are* the divine image. The divine image is a reflection of the apophatic in the kataphatic.

So now we have God transcendent, as omnipresent non-created Reality beyond images (the apophatic God), and we have God immanent, as divine plan expressing throughout created reality, filling empty time and space with an infinity of souls who are God's living, evolving images or self-reflections (the kataphatic God). In our true self, we *are* those living images or self-reflections of God. The divine image is the pre-existing plan and structure for creation's perfection, which is the non-created God's self-expression and mirror-reflection. We humans are created, within and without, in the divine image of God's self-expression. What a gift of eternal blessing to us!

This divine image is contained and reflected in each human soul. That is, we are made in the "image and likeness" of God's self-expression, i.e., in male and female physical bodies outwardly, and in our soul's inner structure and divine potential. God's image is the visible form or structure of the Tree in us and God's likeness is what the form is designed to contain; that is, God's likeness consists of the divine attitudes, qualities and consciousness meant to eventually express through the form as each soul evolves into the fullness of its life in Christ. Thus, the progressive unfolding of created reality happens on different levels of consciousness and expression that are mapped out on the Tree of Life, which is the practical means for manifesting God's divine plan. As stated earlier, the Tree of Life glyph is an ancient map of consciousness covering all levels of created reality.

It's been said that in the beginning God created humans in God's image and likeness, and we've been returning the compliment ever since with poor results; that is, we've been creating God in our unevolved images and likenesses, ascribing to God some of our own flawed attitudes and characteristics. These images and interpretations of God are our own limited ideals and unconscious projections. Hence, our ideas of God are not God; at best, they accurately point toward the uncreated reality of God. Since the non-created divine is apophatic, it may be represented by any number of kataphatic images. The Tree of Life is one of these, as are the Trinity and the Cross.

3

THE SUPERNAL TRIAD

According to my sources,[1] the Secret Wisdom of Israel, which consists of Qabalah and the Tree of Life, was given to humanity over six thousand years ago by the angels as a way of return to God. The Tree of Life glyph is a master symbol consisting of ten Spheres, called "Sephiroth," that are arranged in three vertical columns or pillars known as the Pillar of Severity, the Middle Pillar and the Pillar of Mercy. The Middle Pillar has four Sephiroth on it and the two side pillars have three Sephiroth each. Each of the ten Sephiroth is a specific Sphere of emanation and activity of the divine universal-consciousness and each has particular functions on the Tree of Life. The highest Sephira, at the top of the Middle Pillar, is called "Kether, the Crown." This Sphere is the first emanation of the apophatic *ain soph aur* or Limitless Light of non-created Reality (God transcendent).

Kether/Crown is the One, the indivisible light of Universal-Consciousness permeating the Tree of Life and all of created reality. It is an absolute consciousness, meaning that it is one with all creation and nothing exists apart from the Universal-Consciousness of Kether, the Crown. Kether and its Limitless Light are "the King of kings and Lord of lords, who alone has immortality, and who dwells in unapproachable light, and whom no human being has seen or can see," as mentioned by Paul in 1 Timothy 6:16. This Divine-Light Consciousness of non-created Reality is "unapproachable" or "inaccessible" because it is absolutely one with everything in created reality and consequently may not be perceived, approached or known as a separate thing. Beyond all perspectives of ego-consciousness, nothing is or may be apart from God's omnipresent awareness through Kether/Crown, though most microcosmic units (souls) of evolving consciousness and life are quite unconscious of this.

The Tree of Life has been called "ten in One." Kether/Crown is this One, which invisibly pervades the entire Tree and all of creation. It is in Kether that we have the original inspiration or idea for creation and "the beginning of the whirling" of creation's energies. The whirling of creation's energies continues all the way down the Tree and is expressed in the physical Universe, called "Malkuth/Kingdom," throughout Nature, as in the motions of planets, solar systems, stars, galaxies, molecules, atoms and the tiniest quantum particles.

The inconceivable spinning motion in Kether on the highest spiritual level initiates the movement of creation's energies that, like a lightning flash, manifest the Tree of Life and follow their destined path downward in sequence through all the Sephiroth (1 to 10). The intention to create and the image of the divine plan are conceived in Kether by the divine-consciousness. This is the Archetypal World or abstract level where creation begins, the first step taken toward manifesting creation within and out of the Limitless Light.

To move the divine intention and plan forward, the One, the indivisible, creates a division within itself while remaining One and undivided on its own higher level of universal-consciousness joined simultaneously to the Limitless light and created reality. The division of the One into the Two within itself drops creation's primal energy down from the Limitless Light and unity of Kether onto the plane of original duality. As this happens, below Kether, to the right and left, two Sephiroth jump into manifestation at the tops of the right and left pillars of the Tree; these are the Pillar of Mercy (right) and the Pillar of Severity (left). These two Sephiroth are Divine Cosmic Father on the right, known in Qabalah as Chokmah/Wisdom (no. 2), and Divine Cosmic Mother on the left, known as Binah/Understanding (no. 3). These two Sephiroth, together with Kether, form the Supernal Triad, the uppermost triad on the Tree.

Kether/Crown at the top of the Central Pillar constitutes the first world or level of creation, known as the Archetypal World. This is the world of absolute unity, divine inspiration, intention and original, abstract ideas, where the plan for creation is first conceived by the divine consciousness. It is the realm of all possibilities in the divine mind. What it actually is, of course, utterly transcends the limited capacity of our human minds to conceive or imagine. The same holds true for the other two Sephiroth in the Supernal Triad, Chokmah and Binah, who together constitute the Creative World. We may, at best, only vaguely imagine what these Supernal-Triad Sephiroth actually are. They are Two in One, Divine Masculine and Divine Feminine, Father and Mother of all that exists.

The second Sephira, Chokmah/Wisdom (Divine Father), is located at the top of the Pillar of Mercy, on the right side of the Tree. And the third Sephira, Binah/Understanding (Divine Mother), is located at the top of the Pillar of Severity, on the left side of the Tree. Together, Chokmah and Binah constitute the second world or level of creation, the Creative World. This is where the One (Kether/Crown) divides

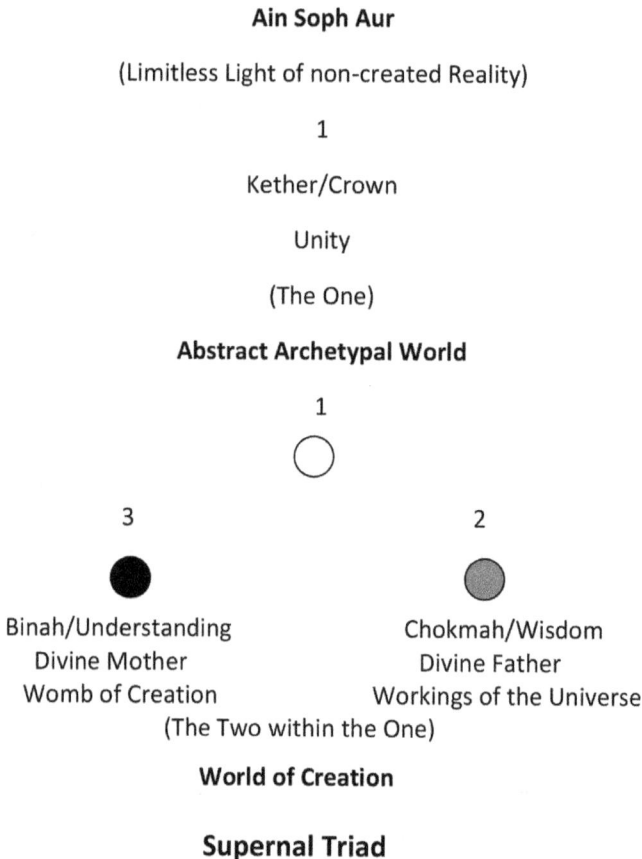

Ain Soph Aur

(Limitless Light of non-created Reality)

1

Kether/Crown

Unity

(The One)

Abstract Archetypal World

1

○

3	2
●	◉
Binah/Understanding	Chokmah/Wisdom
Divine Mother	Divine Father
Womb of Creation	Workings of the Universe

(The Two within the One)

World of Creation

Supernal Triad

into the Two (Chokmah/Wisdom and Binah/Understanding) within itself, in order to manifest the polarities of masculine and feminine energies that are required for creation to happen. Chokmah directs "the workings of the Universe," and Binah is the Universal Womb of Creation where images (projected by Chokmah into Binah) are formed, individual souls are created, and Nature's Laws are fashioned:

Creation always begins and takes place in consciousness. The abstract idea of the divine plan for creation is initially conceived in the Archetypal World, in the unity-consciousness of Kether. Then, in the Creative World, Divine Father and Divine Mother (the "us" in Gen. 1:26) join together in blissful communion and union to create images to express and complete the divine idea from the Archetypal World. In Chokmah/Wisdom (Divine Father), the whirling energies from Kether are organized on an invisible level by imagination so they can become forms. In Binah/Understanding (Divine Mother), the invisible images released from Chokmah enter the enclosure of her womb and are solidified into form-patterns by the limiting, formative feminine principle of creation that concentrates and condenses their energies into fixed structures or shapes.

The creative imagination of Chokmah determines the kinds of forms that will be developed on the Tree of Life, and Binah, the Divine Feminine, gives them their actual shapes or structures. Here we have a general description of the origins of creation on the highest spiritual levels, i.e., the Archetypal and Creative Worlds within the Supernal Triad at the top of the Tree where what happens between Chokmah and Binah is analogous to what happens far below in human procreation between the sperm and the egg of a man and a woman. The expansive, imaginative power of Chokmah conceives the abstract ideas received from Kether into images, and the limiting, concentrative power of Binah embraces those images, projected from Chokmah into her womb, and gives them their actual shapes or forms. Binah, Divine Mother, is the Universal Womb of Creation within which all that is originates and exists. Binah is the ultimate container or what Thomas Keating has called "the womb of God."

Every womb is an enclosure for the condensation and shaping of creative energies. Hence, enclosing, concentrating, focusing and limiting are all characteristics of Binah and the creative Feminine Principle. The invisible images of Chokmah (Divine Father) have to be captured, confined, concentrated and directed, if they're to coalesce into fixed particular images. Here we may see the fundamental characteristics of the Masculine and Feminine Principles of creation: The masculine Chokmah is expansive and imaginative, able to capture any abstract thought or archetype and transmit it as an invisible image into the womb of Binah, the divine feminine. Upon receiving the loose, spinning invisible energy from Chokmah's imaginative power, Binah encloses it in her womb, to condense and shape it into a fixed image or form via concentration. These are universal principles of creativity, which always requires both the expansive, imaginative Masculine Principle and the receptive, concentrating Feminine Principle to produce anything new or original out of what already exists.

All of creation in the Supernal Triad, and throughout the Tree of Life, is happening within God's consciousness, within the absolute unity-consciousness of Kether/Crown, grounded in the Limitless Light of non-created Reality. The images formed through the interactions of energies between Divine Father (Chokmah) and Divine Mother (Binah) in the World of Creation form the symbolic "blueprint" of what is required for the divine plan to take form and expression. From the Supernal Triad, this plan and its images must move down through the next two triads of the Tree so they may finally out-manifest in the physical body and Universe. "Formation" and "Manifestation" are the names of the remaining two Worlds on the Tree of Life under the Archetypal World and the World of Creation in the Supernal Triad.

4

THE SPIRITUAL / MORAL TRIAD

The next phase in the movements of energies and consciousness down the Tree from the Supernal Triad is the transition from there into the World of Formation. The World of Formation occupies a large space on the Tree and is made up of two Triads, the Spiritual Triad (also called the Moral/Ethical Triad) and the lower Personality Triad (also called the Astral Triad). Below, we have represented the upper half of the World of Formation, the Spiritual/Moral Triad.

The Spiritual/Moral Triad is the triad of universal spiritual values and our soul's individual spiritual ground; the Supernal Triad above it is the soul's origin in Divine Mother and its universal spiritual ground. The spiritual ideals and laws of the divine plan, as they relate to individual souls, are formed in the Spiritual/Moral Triad. These ideals are based on the principle of Universal Love and the Laws of Cosmic Justice, which are based on the inner oneness and unconditional love of all individual souls in the One God as Father, Son and Holy Spirit (see diagram on next page). In Qabalah, the Holy Spirit correlates to Binah, the Divine Mother in whom all individual souls are formed and born as miniature microcosmic replicas of the Universal Macrocosm or Tree of Life.

The principles of universal love, compassion and forgiveness arise and issue forth in the World of Formation from the fourth Sephira, Chesed/Mercy, located on the Tree immediately below Chokmah, in the middle of the right-side Pillar of Mercy. Chesed, the blue Sephira, is the origin and inspiration of altruism, forgiveness and spiritual idealism. It is the higher, intuitive mind that

5	4
Geburah/Severity	Chesed/Mercy
Conscience	Spiritual Idealism
(Justice, Fear, Strength)	(Love, Compassion, Forgiveness)

6

Tiphareth/Beauty

(Messiah/Redeemer)

Christ/Son of God

(soul's divine indwelling)

Upper World of Formation – Spiritual/Moral Triad

grasps the hidden mysteries of creation and is one with the universal spiritual qualities and values of love, truth and freedom for all. Chesed partakes of the Wealth of Wisdom, which flows down into it directly via the energy path linking it to Chokmah/Wisdom in the Supernal Triad. Chesed, the Merciful, pours its sacred energies down into Christ, the Son (Tiphareth/Beauty), via the energy path linking Chesed to Tiphareth in the center of the Tree. Chesed represents the highest form of expression to which human consciousness may attain on the personality level. It is the level of unconditional love, compassion and forgiveness for all.

The Laws of Cosmic Justice are formed and expressed in the fiery energy of the red, fifth Sephira, Geburah/Severity, located in the middle of the Pillar of Severity opposite Chesed on the left side of the Tree immediately below Binah, Divine Mother. The Hebrew word for "justice," *pahad*, also means "fear." "Fear" in Geburah/Severity means not only fear and anxiety regarding the consequences of our errors or sins, but also the soul's deep sense of awe and reverence toward God. Geburah is associated with discrimination or right judgment in the evaluation of choices; and Geburah is also the source of our inner voice of conscience. Geburah administers the Laws of Cosmic Justice (called "karma" in Eastern Traditions) which work to maintain and restore harmony and balance in created reality.

The purpose of these laws is not to punish the soul but to correct and teach it, to create inner balance so we may live and grow in harmony with the spiritual qualities and values of our true self (divine image). The negative effects of these laws come into play when we fail to hear and heed the inner voice of conscience, which is the voice of divine guidance and wisdom God has placed in our soul. The presence and functioning of Geburah, which discriminates between good and evil, is a primary reason why our soul's individual Spiritual Triad has also been called "the Moral/Ethical Triad." Geburah is in service to the higher values of Chesed and is the faithful moral/ethical compass in our soul.

The inner path of Geburah, followed in humility and harmony with our true conscience, is the path to spiritual victory in our soul's confrontations and struggles with temptations and evil. Other key attributes of Geburah are "strength" (in the sense of moral/ethical integrity), volition or will power, action and the soul's reproductive energies—which are life-giving when respected but become destructive when abused. Geburah is in direct reception of the energies and consciousness of Binah/Understanding, at the top of the Feminine Pillar. The quality and power of foresight is one of the key attributes of Binah, and this is given directly to Geburah by Divine Mother via the energy path that links them.

Consequently, one of the virtues or powers of our true conscience is the ability to know intuitively in advance what the positive or negative consequences will be of any choice or action we consider. This is especially important in cases involving moral/ethical decisions that affect the inner harmony, health and wellbeing of our soul. Hence, two key words associated with Geburah are judgment (as in exercising "good judgment") and fear/justice (as in the positive or negative spiritual consequences of our moral/ethical choices). Geburah's fiery energy drives and motivates us to action, and one of our primary challenges as human beings and spiritual beings is learning how to consciously handle and constructively direct Geburah's creative powers or sexual energies in ways that are in harmony with true conscience and higher spiritual values.

Like Chesed, Geburah pours its qualities, energy and consciousness down into the divine Son, Tiphareth, on the Middle Pillar in the center of the Tree, via the energy path connecting them. Hence, the Son of God is filled with the love of justice and righteousness characteristic of Geburah. The two Sephiroth on the side Pillars that bear their names, Mercy and Severity, together express the primary governing principles of the Spiritual/Moral Triad and our soul's inner spiritual ground. Tiphareth, the yellow sixth Sephira in the center below them, is the key Sephira that works to activate and integrate these higher principles, energies and qualities into the Personality/Astral Triad, and from there into the physical World of Manifestation (Malkuth). Thus, it's through Christ or Tiphareth that the divine plan for created reality may be fulfilled.

In addition to the two energy paths from Chesed and Geburah connecting into Tiphareth to form the Spiritual/Moral Triad, three more energy paths pour into Tiphareth from the higher-up Spheres of the Supernal Triad: Kether, Chokmah and Binah. It's important to remember here that each Sephira on the Tree of Life is an emanation and sphere of activity of the one Universal-Consciousness, i.e., Kether/Limitless Light (to separate Kether from the Limitless Light is a dualistic concept). Hence, the various Sephiroth, though outwardly distinct, are inwardly not separate from one another or from the Limitless Light.

Kether, the indivisible, is the One "I am" of the Universal Self who famously spoke to Moses from the "burning bush," saying, "I am who I am" (Ex. 3:14). Tiphareth/Beauty, the Word or begotten Son of God, is likewise identified with the Universal Self and also the "I am" or true self of each individual soul in created reality. Tiphareth is God's self-reflection in us and in created reality, i.e., Tiphareth, in its aspects as Word of God and God the Son, is the fullness and perfection of God's divine image in created reality.

Tiphareth, as the fullness and perfection of the divine image, is God's self-reflection in the World of Formation. This self-reflection, called "Beauty," is the summation of Tiphareth, the Son, plus the divine energies and qualities poured into Tiphareth from the first five Sephiroth on the Tree, i.e., Kether, Chokmah, Binah, Chesed and Geburah. The first five Sephiroth may be compared to prism-rays expressing primary aspects of the Limitless Light that come together and reunite in the integral Son-ray, Tiphareth, to form the perfected divine image. This perfected divine image is the highest evolutionary potential of each soul that may be realized, by God's grace, through the fullness of its rebirth and life in Christ.

The first ray from Limitless Light is Kether/Crown, the most brilliant white light of unity containing all colors and consciousness. The other two members of the Supernal Triad are Chokmah/Wisdom, colored gray (representing the union of opposites), and Binah/Understanding, colored black or dark violet (representing the dark womb of creation). The three Sephiroth of the Spiritual/Moral Triad, Chesed, Geburah and Tiphareth, emanate the three primary colors whence all colors may be produced. Chesed is blue, Geburah red and Tiphareth, the Son, is yellow. As all the higher Sephiroth pour their energies, qualities and consciousness into it, Tiphareth is the consummation in the upper World of Formation of the divine creative impulse originated in the Limitless Light, i.e., Tiphareth, the Son, is the invisible, non-created God's visible self-reflection, the One we adore.

Chokmah, Divine Father, and Binah, Divine Mother, are the heavenly parents of God the Son, i.e., Tiphareth, in created reality. In these three, Chokmah, Tiphareth and Binah, we have a Qabalistic expression of the Christian Trinity (Father, Son and Holy Spirit), Three Persons in One God: the One, of course, being Kether, the Crown-consciousness of absolute Unity which cannot be realized or perceived as a separate thing. God's descent into the World of Formation as Tiphareth, the divine Son, is the next essential step in the process of carrying the divine plan for created reality forward. All the virtues, qualities and powers of the heavenly divine, i.e., the first five Sephiroth, are invested in Tiphareth the Son, the Christ and most beautiful holy one of God.

In the Prologue of John's Gospel, we read: "In the beginning was the Word, and the Word was with God, and the Word was God. He was in the beginning with God. All things came into being through him, and without him not one thing came into being. What has come into being in him was life, and the life was the light of all people. The light shines in the darkness, and the darkness did not overcome it.... The true light which enlightens everyone was coming into the world.... To all who received him, who believed in his name, he gave power to become children of God, who were born, not of blood or of the will of the flesh or of the will of man, but of God. And the Word became flesh and lived among us, and we have seen his glory, the glory as of a father's only son, full of grace and truth" (John 1:1–5, 9, 12–14).

This New Testament creation story is, in my humble view, a perfect Qabalistic description of the Christ (Tiphareth/Beauty), the anointed one and only begotten Son of God who dwells in the true center and heart of all souls. A word about the Lord's "name," mentioned above: in Qabalah, to name something is to give it its characteristics. To "believe in the Lord's name" is to believe in more than just a word, in whatever language. To believe in the Lord's name is to believe, deeply believe, in his characteristics and true identity, as God, the divine principle in the human soul and Lord of all creation, whether we call it "Tiphareth," "Christ," or something else. It is what it is, no matter what we call it.

The ancient Qabalistic teachings anticipated the birth of Christ into the chosen people of God's human family. The Hebrew word for him, of course, is not "Christ," which comes from the Greek "Christos," meaning "the anointed one of God." Tiphareth is also known in Hebrew as "Ben," the Son, of Chokmah, who is called "Ab," the Father. The primary function of "Ben," the Son, is to do the will of "Ab," the Father. Hence, Tiphareth is also called "the anointed one" and, in Hebrew, the "mechhiah," which means "messiah," the redeemer and savior. "Christ" is the English word for this.

Some of the other ancient Qabalistic attributions of Tiphareth are as follows: Prince of Peace ("Shalom"), which implies perfection and wholeness; Mystical Redeemer; Image-Making Power (derived from Chokmah and Binah); Separating Intelligence (derived from Binah and Geburah); Sun (in the sense of each soul's inner spiritual Sun); and Adam, meaning generic humanity and all living things (in Genesis 3:20, we read that "The man," Adam, "named his wife Eve because she was the mother of all living."). This has implications extending far beyond the human family. The paradox of Tiphareth, the Son, being both Christ and Adam: as God, the Son, and as fallen humanity, arises from the reality of Christ as God's eternal Word and only begotten Son being also united to the evolving human family as the redeeming divine indwelling in each individual soul. This is one of the great wonders and mysteries of the Mystical Body of Christ.

So Tiphareth, the yellow sixth Sephira and centerpiece on the Tree, is the creative focal point of both the Spiritual/Moral Triad and the Supernal Triad, i.e., of the entire upper half of the Tree. Everything from above, from the Supernal and Spiritual/Moral Triads, pours into Tiphareth because Tiphareth *is* the Word of God through whom and out of whom the entire manifested Universe (visible and invisible) is created. In Tiphareth is the culmination of the first five Sephiroth. Tiphareth is the pivotal turning point whence the energy of Spirit (Divine Mother) descends into denser formations in the Personality/Astral Triad, and, from there, into the outer physical World of Manifestation (Malkuth/Kingdom), whence begins the process of our evolution back up the Tree. Tiphareth, as divine Word and Son, and as the inner light (Sun) in every soul, is also known, in English, as the "Christ-Consciousness."

So Tiphareth, the Son, is invested with all the goods from above. All the treasures of heaven, held by the first five Sephiroth, are poured into the "anointed one," "mechhia," the Christ, so that the Son is whole and complete in Word and Image, in power and preciousness, full in all virtues of wisdom and truth, love and righteousness. From Binah, Divine Mother, the womb of creation is poured into the Son, through whom all things in the World of Manifestation come into being. The first five Sephiroth and Tiphareth, in whom they all meet, are the divine action in each soul and throughout the Universe of created reality. Tiphareth is the shining sun of glory in the heart of creation and in the true center of every soul. What else could the Son and divine-image reflection of non-created Reality be but Beauty, the finest, highest ideal of the non-created God's self-expression?

More than any other Sephira, Tiphareth is multifaceted; that is, has a number of roles to play and functions to perform in service of the divine plan. This is why Tiphareth, who connects the above with the below, has such a variety of different names and attributions. In addition to "Adam," generic humanity, another important name for Tiphareth in the individual soul is the "Central Self," "Higher Self," or "divine indwelling." We may, of course, also call Tiphareth in the individual soul our "true self," the term used in Centering Prayer's conceptual background.

Each name or attribution of Tiphareth carries with it a particular role or function that is essential for activating and furthering the divine plan, i.e., the will of "Ab," the Father—from whom, incidentally, Abraham received his name as the father of God's chosen people through whom the Son was destined to incarnate into the human family. Today, God's chosen people are all who seek God because we are all part of the divine and the divine dwells in each of us as our Higher Self. The term, "Higher Self," applied to Tiphareth in the individual soul, also applies to Kether/Crown as the Universal Higher Self. These two are ultimately one and the same in the non-dual consciousness of Kether and Limitless Light.

5

THE PERSONALITY/ASTRAL TRIAD

I

On the universal macrocosmic scale, Christ, the Son, is responsible for the formative and manifesting stages of God's creation below the Spiritual/Moral Triad. That is, it's a function of God's Word, Tiphareth, to carry forward the divine plan into the Personality/Astral Triad (the lower half of the World of Formation), and from there into the outer, physical World of Manifestation, the tenth Sephira, Malkuth/Kingdom. The Supernal Triad (Kether, Chokmah and Binah) is responsible for the archetypal idea, inspiration, vision and creative design of the plan, i.e., its original architecture, and Christ, the Son, is then the builder of what the Father, Chokmah, and Mother, Binah (inspired by Kether) intend and design. An essential part of the divine plan involves personal free will and the evolution of individual souls (represented by Adam) from the human ground of Malkuth and the Personality Astral Triad up into the spiritual ground of the divine indwelling, i.e., Tiphareth and the Spiritual/Moral Triad.

On the individual microcosmic scale, Christ, the Son, serves as the personal savior of each individual soul-personality in the forms of its conscience and true self or spiritual identity. What happens in the course of our inner unfolding under the divine plan is that the Spiritual/Moral Triad within us, through the active agency of Christ (Tiphareth) and with our willing consent and active cooperation, redeems the Personality/Astral Triad by bringing its human-ground expression into alignment and harmony with the qualities and values of the soul's spiritual ground. This is essentially how the divine plan is fulfilled in each soul.

Tiphareth/Beauty, who is Christ and God, the Son, plays the central role in making our human personality and evolving soul into "a new creation" (2 Cor. 5:17). The purpose of this "new creation," of course, is to express the divine image present in Tiphareth, our divine true self, in the denser energy field of our personality and outer expression in human ground. Because we are given the great gift of free will, the divine plan may be fulfilled in us only when it becomes our strongest desire, highest ideal and deepest purpose in life. Only then will we have the dedication, inspiration and motivation to fully consent and cooperate with the process of our rebirth in Christ, which involves our inner transformation from false self into true self.

On the following page is a diagram representing Tiphareth in relation to the Personality/Astral Triad and the Qabalistic World of Manifestation, Malkuth/Kingdom. From this diagram, we may visualize the energy paths connecting Tiphareth to the three Sephiroth of the Personality/Astral Triad and Malkuth, at the bottom of the Tree's Middle Pillar. It is through these energy paths that Tiphareth works, with our consent and cooperation, upon the personality or false self, to purify, heal, refine and eventually transform it into a living expression of the divine image. In the following diagram, we may also visualize the energy paths connecting the Sephiroth of the Personality/Astral Triad, which are in continual interaction with one another, creating our thoughts, feelings, perceptions, subconscious activities and patterns. Malkuth/Kingdom, the physical body at the bottom of the Tree, is in reception of all the energies that come down from the Personality/Astral Triad above it via the energy paths connecting them. Our physical-brain consciousness in Malkuth is directly affected by the activities of the Sephiroth above it, by the physical environment, and by various bio-chemical activities within the physical body, brain and nervous system.

6

Tiphareth/Beauty

Bottom of Spiritual/Moral Triad and Upper World of Formation

◯

8	7
Hod/Splendor	Netzach/Victory
Intellect	Emotions, Imagination
◯	◯
Reason, Logic, Concepts	Images, Will, Desire Nature
(Lower Concrete Mind)	(Full Range of Feelings)

9

Yesod/Foundation

Instinctual Nature, Subconscious Mind

●

Vital Animal Soul, Psychic Awareness

(Memory, Habit Patterns, Automatic Consciousness)

(Individual and Collective Unconscious)

Lower World of Formation

10

Malkuth/Kingdom

●

Physical Body and Universe

(Physical-brain consciousness and senses)

(Physical Time, Space and Substance)

World of Manifestation

Personality/Astral Triad with Tiphareth above and Malkuth/Kingdom below

II

As creation's energies and images are projected down the Tree through its successive Sephiroth, Triads and Worlds, they become increasingly dense and solid, culminating in the gross physical matter we experience in Malkuth, the World of Manifestation. This is a gradual movement of created reality's energy and ideas from their most abstract origins in Kether, Chokmah and Binah down into their most concrete expressions in Malkuth. Between these extremes are several gradations of energy-becoming-substance in which the whirling energies of Kether and Chokmah gradually grow more concentrated, confined, solidified and fixed. Prior to and just above the physical matter of Malkuth are various gradations of subtle "astral matter" in the Personality/Astral Triad, each Sphere of which is a vast domain (like the physical Universe) inhabited by a diverse variety of nonphysical beings and centers of consciousness. (See diagram on next page.)

The Personality/Astral Triad is the triad of our individual human ground. The feelings, images, ideas and forms that take shape in this Triad are living structures made up of what's been called "astral matter." This is why we're calling it the "Personality/Astral Triad." For simplicity's sake, we're using the term *astral* to include the wide range of energies and forms (including feelings, thoughts, impulses, habit-patterns, memories and consciousness) that are expressed in the Personality/Astral Triad. These are all made up of different gradations of subtle "astral matter" that encompass the varied activities and manifestations of the three interconnected Sephiroth in the Personality/Astral Triad: Netzach/Victory, Hod/Splendor and Yesod/Foundation.

The seventh, green Sephira, Netzach/Victory, at the foot of the right-side Masculine Pillar, under Chesed/Mercy, is the Sephira of our desire nature, which includes our will, imagination and emotions. A central part of our personal human drama involves free will choices, what we want in life and whether or not we get what we want. As we learn and grow, our desires change as new wants are discovered and old ones are outgrown. As this happens, changes occur in the subtle astral matter of our desire nature. We have human desires and spiritual desires, desires of our false self and of our true self. We have inborn instinctual desires (our basic instinctual needs), and we have learned desires—so many desires.

Desires come to us from three basic sources: heredity, environment and our higher spiritual nature, which is, in a non-biological sense, also hereditary. Our non-spiritual hereditary desires are those that arise from our animal nature and instinctual needs for security/survival/safety, sensation/pleasure, affection/esteem/approval, power/control and, to some extent, intimacy/belonging (which is also our higher spiritual need for love and relationship to the divine). Our hereditary instinctual desires and their distortions into emotional happiness programs help to form our personality and are housed in the ninth Sephira, Yesod/Foundation, as subconscious patterns, memories and desires. Our environmental desires, which come primarily from social learning and cultural conditioning, also play a major role in shaping our personality, values and worldview in human ground.

The higher spiritual desires that arise in Netzach come to us from the Spiritual/Moral Triad in our soul, i.e., Tiphareth, Geburah and Chesed. Higher spiritual desires, such as those of true conscience and altruistic compassion, are initially transmitted into Netzach through its connection to Tiphareth. The higher attribution of Netzach as "Victory" refers to our spiritual victory over needless human suffering and the false self; and it refers to the fulfillment of the higher spiritual desires in our soul. "Spiritual Victory" ultimately means the shifting of our center of consciousness and identity from our false self to our true self in Christ (Tiphareth). A restructuring of our desire nature and its subconscious patterns in Yesod, in accord with the light of true conscience and divine love, is required for our spiritual identity-shift and rebirth in Christ to occur.

Desires are conceived in Netzach as images that are charged with the energy of our emotions and will power. The force of these desires circulates among the Sephiroth of the Personality/Astral Triad, as well as into Malkuth (our physical body). It's desire that motivates us to action on all levels and in whichever directions we incline. The soul's desires are intimately related to its basic instinctual needs, appetites, and pursuits of freedom, happiness and whatever aspirations or dreams we envision and hope to accomplish. Desire is a fire burning in the soul. It's our motivational fuel.

Since our desires may originate from different sources with opposing inclinations, there is not always harmony among them. Human desires are often in conflict and this tends to divide one's energy and disturb our peace of mind. Ambivalence, conflict and uncertainty regarding what we want are common experiences we all encounter. In addition to its higher spiritual meaning, the term *victory* is appropriate for Netzach because victory means getting what we want; and (like Chokmah and Binah in the Supernal Triad) whatever images we charge with the energy of our desire and will power shall inevitably manifest in some way at some time. Often there's irony in this on the human level because our "victory" of getting what we wanted may not be what we want when we actually do get it! For example, what we wanted as an infant or child, and may still desire unconsciously, is often not what we want as an adult, e.g., false self's emotional happiness programs that can bring so much unhappiness.

As mentioned above, a key part of human and spiritual growth involves the purification and redirection of our desire nature and its unconscious habit-patterns—which form a major part of our personality's automatic, subconscious programming of feelings, desires, thoughts and actions. Purifying our desire nature involves not only changing what we desire; it also requires changing the inner attitudes and motivations with which we pursue our desires, i.e., the spirit in which we act. Attitudes of the false self tend to proceed from self-centered perspectives that give lower priority to the rights and needs of others whereas attitudes that express the true self tend to come from an inner presence or orientation of peace, kindness, compassion, goodwill and respect for the rights and needs of others.

Inspiration for refining and elevating our motivations and desires flows down into Netzach and the other two Sephiroth of the Personality/Astral Triad through the energy paths connecting them to Tiphareth and the Spiritual/Moral Triad. This happens when, in humility and faith, we are open and receptive to higher spiritual influences. Higher energies, ideals and inspirations are transmitted to our personality and desire nature from Tiphareth, the Central Sephira, and from Chesed, immediately above Netzach. These higher energies and ideals activate changes in our desire nature and the other Sephiroth of the Personality/Astral Triad, which in turn act and react upon one another in a circular motion in accord with our desires (personal will) and levels of conscious and unconscious cooperation with the divine action.

III

Netzach/Victory is the Sephira of emotions, motivations and desires. Our desire nature in Netzach is directly affected by signals coming up from our physical body, senses and relationships in Malkuth, by a continual flow of input from our memories, associations and subconscious habit-patterns in Yesod, and by thoughts and ideas coming from our intellect in Hod/Splendor. This is part of how the Sephiroth in human ground (Personality/Astral Triad and Malkuth) interact with one another. As desires become conscious, we tend to think about them. This happens when images of our desires in Netzach are communicated to our intellect in Hod, the eighth orange Sephira, via the horizontal energy path connecting them. Thoughts circulate around the images of our desires held in the intellect, elaborating upon them in reflections, fantasies and analysis. Hod is located at the foot of the Feminine Pillar, on the left side of the Tree opposite Netzach, directly underneath Geburah, with Binah above. Hod/Splendor is the mental Sephira in our Personality/Astral Triad and human ground.

As feelings and desires in Netzach are influenced by the adjacent Sephiroth, so are the thought and reasoning processes in Hod directly influenced by input from Malkuth and the other two Sephiroth in the Personality/Astral Triad. In fact, all the Sephiroth on the Tree of Life are continually interacting with one another and exchanging energies. This is expressive of the fact that the soul is a multi-dimensional energy field of living forces that may function both harmoniously and inharmoniously in relation to one another on both conscious and unconscious levels. The intellect in Hod may also be influenced by the Sephiroth above it in the Spiritual/Moral Triad.

The intellect's clarity and understanding increase as its consciousness awakens into recognition of inner guidance from Tiphareth, the Son. This helps the relationship between the personality and the true self to develop. How our intellect reasons depends on the influences it receives from the other Spheres in the Personality/Astral Triad (Netzach and Yesod), from the physical body and environment (Malkuth), and on whether or not it's open and receptive to inner guidance from the Higher Self in Tiphareth and the Spiritual/Moral Triad. In its least evolved state, the intellect is driven by subconscious patterns, impulses and energies in Yesod, by random emotions and desires in Netzach, and by stimulations coming from the physical body and environment in Malkuth. Hence, finding inner peace, balance and harmony is a challenge we all need to address if we're to "get our house in order" and enjoy inner wellbeing.

We might also call the Personality/Astral Triad the "Separate-self Triad," since it's the Tree-of-Life Triad in which our separate-self perceptions and false self arise. This self, our personality and separate-self, is the primary self we know and identify with in human ground. It's a false self because it's not who we truly are as spiritual beings created in the divine image. It's in our intellect that we perceive our separate-self in relation to others and what's around us. Hod (the intellect) is the place in the Personality/Astral Triad where the human ego reflects itself to itself as the separate-self. On a lower level, this is analogous to God's divine self-reflection in Tiphareth and the Spiritual/Moral Triad. Our separate ego-identity tends to do a lot of self-reflecting in the mental mirror of intellect (Hod); and one of the chief bastions of the false self is over-identification with the intellect, mistaking if for whom we are rather than seeing it as a tool we have and use.

Hod is our lower, concrete mind that reflects our separate human existence to us as it collects, organizes and categorizes information. Our human intellect is essentially an instrument of limitation, reflection, focus and concentration that holds and duplicates whatever enters it. Analogous to Binah, the Divine Mother and Universal Womb of Creation, the intellect contains, concentrates, forms and analyzes whatever it works upon. Through its cognitive labors, Hod gives birth to a variety of intellectual opinions, reflections, conclusions, views, judgments and insights of certainty and uncertainty. Chesed/Mercy, on the other hand, is our higher, intuitive mind that may, through the agency of Tiphareth, inspire Hod to more creative, uplifting and original ideas.

Our lower mind is naturally given to linear, dualistic, "either/or" thinking and to literal, "common sense" interpretations of whatever it perceives. Hod works at putting thoughts into words and at drawing conclusions from the information it collects, using inductive or deductive logic based on assumptions. With the help of metaphors, higher mathematics, images from Netazch and higher inspirations from the Spiritual/Moral Triad, our limited human intellect may learn to think more broadly and abstractly than it initially does on its own. To become truly creative, our intellect needs to be "impregnated" by intuition. This is similar to how Binah, Divine Mother in the Supernal Triad, needs to be "impregnated" with the original ideas and images for creation generated by Chokmah, Divine Father.

Our intellect is a means to an end, not an end in itself. To use our intellect freely and intelligently, we need to understand that it's a limited instrument and not our true identity. Our intellect is not self-sufficient but dependent on input from outside itself, i.e., input from the neighboring Sephiroth that connect and send energy into it. As mentioned above, these Sephiroth include Yesod and Netzach in the Personality/Astral Triad, Malkut below, and the Spiritual/Moral Triad above.

When the higher influence from Tiphareth is consciously perceived in the intellect, this helps it to expand into higher levels of awareness and receptivity to the Spiritual/Moral Triad. These contacts can elevate, refine and transform the intellect into an instrument in service to spiritual growth. As the intellect's awareness becomes more elevated, broad and refined by influences from the Spiritual/Moral Triad, it naturally becomes more integrated, whole and intelligent. As Hod is transformed by higher influences, it's able to focus more precisely and to see more clearly than when it was simply reacting blindly and automatically to unconscious patterns and desires coming from Yesod and Netzach in the Personality/Astral Triad, or from outside environmental input.

As the intellect is refined, its activities may help to refine the desires in Netzach and the subconscious patterns in Yesod. This, of course, contributes significantly to the spiritual healing and rebirth of the personality. It's important to bear in mind here that this inner work of transformation in the intellect, and in Yesod and Netzach, takes place and is accomplished, with our cooperation and support, by the divine action of Tiphareth, the Son or divine indwelling working in the soul. Tiphareth (The Central Sephira) is like an alchemical caldron or mixing bowl for all the energies of the Tree of Life, drawing down energies from the Spheres above it in the Spiritual/Moral and Supernal Triads, and drawing up energies from below in the Personality/Astral Triad, and perhaps even from Malkuth (our physical organism). As Christ came down and was born on Earth in the person of Jesus, so does he, as Tiphareth/Beauty, descend from the Spiritual/Moral Triad and enter into our Personality/Astral Triad for the purpose of healing, renewing, awakening and transforming us. This is the basic process of our inner redemption, resurrection and rebirth in Christ.

The intellect is stimulated and activated by images received from the desire nature in Netzach and, when open to them, by energies and inclinations that may flow down into it from the fiery red Sephira, Geburah, immediately above it on the Feminine Pillar. These energies and influences from Netzach and Geburah stimulate the reasoning process, keeping it active, moving and out of mechanical ruts. The intellect's true splendor shines when it's impregnated with higher inspiration from the Spiritual/Moral Triad. When the intellect focuses on higher ideals and is receptive to them, it naturally draws higher inspirations into itself. Whatever our intellect focuses upon, it will attract more of the same, for better or worse.

The intellect's understanding grows as its awareness grows. Informed by conscience (Geburah) and the spiritual influences from Tiphareth, the mind learns to distinguish between behavior patterns and goals that are healthy, productive and conducive to spiritual growth, and those that are not. It is particularly liberating when the individual learns that her or his true identity is not in the intellect or Personality/Astral Triad, but in the higher, Central

Self in Tiphareth. Then the intellect may be used more freely and effectively as an instrument.

Ultimately, our true mind is not the intellect, but our higher, intuitive mind in Chesed, which expresses the highest spiritual ideals and values. This higher, intuitive mind may reflect from Chesed, in the Spiritual/Moral Triad, down into Hod via Tiphareth, which has energy paths connecting to Chesed and Hod in a straight line running through Tiphareth, i.e., the path from Chesed to Tiphareth and the path from Tiphareth to Hod. When this connection between Chesed and Hod is established, the intellect is uplifted, refined and inspired by the higher energies, ideals and consciousness that descend into it. This is a major transforming event for the intellect, causing its true "Splendor" to awaken and shine.

IV

Yesod/Foundation, the ninth, purple Sephira, is particularly mysterious and interesting. It houses the "Underworld" and archetypes of ancient legends and myth, which correspond to our personal and Collective Unconscious. It is a vast domain (as are all the Sephiroth) holding a variety of nonphysical conscious entities along with the evolutionary history and instinctual energies of all life on Earth. Yesod connects humans to other life forms. In its "animal soul" aspect, Yesod is a subconscious, shared level of instinctual psychic awareness where life-form species are connected, interrelated and communicate on pre-rational levels.

Yesod is also a realm of creation's possibilities where forms are created prior to manifestation in the outer physical world of Malkuth. However, all forms created in Yesod do not out-manifest in physical reality because all are not completed, refined or chosen to be enacted. Yesod, the Sephira of patterns and memory, is where our various psychological habits are lodged, and where the core inner work of contemplation (prayer in secret), involving the soul's purification, healing and renewal, takes place. In fact, the false self or ego in the Personality/Astral Triad cannot be transformed or reborn without changing its unconscious habit-patterns of thought, feeling and action and their living astral-matter structures in Yesod/Foundation.

Yesod is the matrix of our subconscious mind and, like the conscious intellect in Hod, Yesod functions as a natural receiver, container and copy-mechanism. However, unlike the intellect, Yesod possesses a pre-rational innocence that blindly accepts all input it receives without question or discrimination. Yesod is in direct reception from Hod (intellect), Netzach (emotions) and Tiphareth (the divine indwelling). It holds the "master copies" of all habits and patterns in the Personality/Astral Triad. When Yesod receives conflicting messages from within the soul, as it often does, priority tends to be given to those feelings, thoughts, and desires with the most energy or that are supported by the conscious mind.

Yesod stores, processes and reproduces whatever it contains or receives. That is, given an appropriate stimulus, Yesod activates whatever corresponding memory-patterns and habits pre-exist within it; whatever habitually comes into it from surrounding Spheres; as well as whatever impressions and messages it repeatedly receives from the outer world of Malkuth. This process of automatic pattern-activation is simply how our subconscious mind works. Whatever we put into our subconscious is what we'll get back from it. For this reason, discrimination, care and rationing ought to be used in choosing the outer and inner influences to which we expose ourselves.

In Qabalah, Yesod is known as "the Mystical Foundation of Life." Yesod is called "Foundation" because all universal and individual patterns for manifestation in the physical Universe (Malkuth) and in the soul's Personality/Astral Triad are held in Yesod. These patterns are the "master copies" that shape what's reproduced in our body, mind, emotions and consciousness. In order for an individual personality to evolve and become its true self, the "master copies" and subconscious operating system in Yesod that control it need to be upgraded. Hence, the hidden work of the Spirit or divine therapist in each soul's Yesod Sephira is essential for our spiritual growth and rebirth in Christ.

A central aspect of each soul's transformation from false self to true self involves its alignment to true conscience via the purification of habit-patterns in relation to good/evil choices. The

Personality/Astral Triad is the battleground between good and evil in the human soul, as it's here that we are faced with moral/ethical choices and the option of saying "yes" or "no" to life and God's plan. Evil, which necessitates free will, cannot exist or function above the level of the Personality/Astral Triad, though evil's nature is fully recognized, known and understood in Geburah/Severity—the seat of our innate spiritual conscience in the Spiritual/Moral Triad. Evil operates in the shadows of ignorance and unconsciousness in the Personality/Astral Triad, and no such shadows exist in the luminous radiance of the Spiritual/Moral Triad. In the changing light and shadow of life in human ground, evil leads us from the dawn of desire and hope into the twilight of seductive deceptions, giving false promise to emotional happiness programs that cannot possibly work because they don't address our true needs.

Good and evil have both spiritual and terrestrial roots. The spiritual roots of good and evil lie in the basic impetus in creation's energy to return to the Limitless Light of non-created Reality. There are two basic ways for achieving this imperative of return to the Absolute. Good seeks return by way of the divine plan for the evolution of individual souls and consciousness back up the Tree from Malkuth to Kether. From that point, the divine plan aims to bring the divine consciousness of Kether down into Malkuth/Kingdom, so that creation may be fully redeemed and perfected. This plan is to be implemented in individual souls and is obviously an extremely long-term goal that requires our willing consent and dedicated cooperation. Evil, on the other hand, seeks return to non-created Reality by the opposite, shorter route of descent into corruption, chaos, death and destruction. The spiritual origin of the archetypal good/evil conflict in the human soul is the basis of our relative free will, which feels attractions in both directions and is faced with the challenges and choices of saying "yes" or "no" to life, existence and God's divine plan.

The terrestrial or evolutionary roots of good/evil in the human soul come from our inherited instinctual tendencies toward kindness and cruelty, which are harbored in the soul's Yesod/Foundation Sephira as innate subconscious patterns and memories reaching back in time to life's primeval beginnings on Earth. Both kindness and cruelty have grown out of the universal survival instinct in terrestrial life forms. Kindness and caring have originated from the nurturing and care of offspring along with tendencies toward cooperation, shared identity and group loyalty within various species struggling to survive. Cruelty has come from rivalry, competition and the deadly predator-prey activities of carnivores in savage struggles for survival and domination (power/control) among various life-forms.

We humans have inherited tendencies toward both kindness and cruelty from our evolutionary ancestors and, on the conscious level of moral/ethical choices, these translate into conflicts between good and evil in human behavior and relationships, e.g., selfishness versus sharing, peace versus war, honesty versus deception, integrity versus corruption. Tendencies toward both good and evil choices pre-exist in the human soul's inherited primal memory-patterns in the depths of Yesod. Hence, we possess relative free will and the necessity of choosing between good and evil in the conduct of our lives and pursuit of our desires. It's through this inner struggle that our character is forged and our spirit either strengthened or weakened, depending on the moral/ethical caliber of our dominate choices and actions.

V

In addition to "the Mystical Foundation of Life," Yesod has also been called "the sphere of the activity of the union of Divine Father and Divine Mother." This great union occurs below Kether/Crown, on the Middle Pillar of the Tree of Life, in the Supernal Triad where Divine Father (Chokmah) and Divine Mother (Binah) are joined via the energy path connecting them. The immediate product of this divine union is Tiphareth, the Son or Word of God, through whom the Personality/Astral Triad and Malkuth/Kingdom come into being. Tiphareth is also known in Qabalah as "the sphere of the activity of the Sun," i.e., the light that enlightens. The various names and attributes assigned to each of the Sephiroth allow us to see their varied qualities and functions from different angles, each Sephira being an emanation and sphere of activity in and of the One Divine Consciousness (Kether and the Limitless Light of non-created Reality).

We may gain further insight into the Tree of Life by reflecting on the Middle Pillar and some of the salient aspects of the Tree's design and working structure: With Kether/Crown at the top, Tiphareth (corresponding to the Heart Center) is the second Sphere on the Middle Pillar, Yesod (the Sacral Center or Sexual Chakra) is the third and Malkuth (the Root Center) the fourth.* The Middle Pillar forms a direct two-way energy path leading from the bottom to the top of the Tree. This has been called "the Path of the Mystic" (see diagram on following page). Two of the Four Qabalistic Worlds have one Middle-Pillar Sephira: the Archetypal World (Kether) at the top of the Tree and the World of Manifestation (Malkuth) at the bottom. The World of Formation has two Middle-Pillar Spheres (Tiphareth and Yesod in the upper and lower sections respectively); and the World of Creation (with Chokmah and Binah), forming the base of the Supernal Triad, has no visible Sephira on the Middle Pillar.[1]

Additionally, each of the Three Triads on the Tree contains one Middle-Pillar Sephira as follows: Kether in the Supernal Triad, Tiphareth in the Spiritual/Moral Triad and Yesod in the Personality/Astral Triad. Malkuth, at the bottom of the Middle Pillar, stands alone as the outer, physical World of Manifestation, which is the end-product or "fruit" at the bottom of the Tree. The Middle Pillar corresponds to the spinal column in the human body and it's through this key energy-channel that Tiphareth, the Son, may act in and upon Yesod in both microcosm (individual souls) and Macrocosm (the Universe at large). The purpose of this is for Tiphareth to guide the processes and evolution of creation's manifestation from within, and to thereby serve the will of the Father (Chokmah) in both individual souls and the outer Universe.

"The sphere of the activity of the union of Divine Father and Divine Mother" is where the Archetypal Image for created reality (held in Kether, God's unity consciousness) becomes the living universal energy field in Yesod/Foundation that finally forms and prepares God's plan and physical Universe for manifestation in Malkuth/Kingdom. This "descent of spirit into matter" is accomplished

---

* For more on energy centers or chakras on the Tree's Middle Pillar, see endnote 1, chapter 11.

The Path of the Mystic

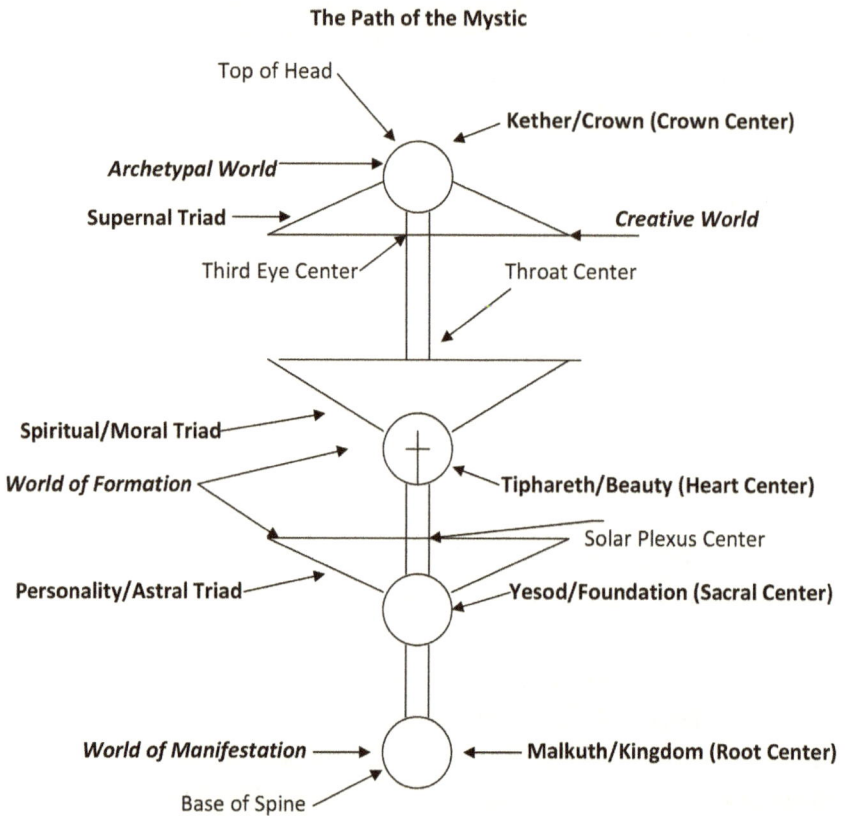

Top of Head

Kether/Crown (Crown Center)

Archetypal World

Supernal Triad

Creative World

Third Eye Center

Throat Center

Spiritual/Moral Triad

World of Formation

Tiphareth/Beauty (Heart Center)

Solar Plexus Center

Personality/Astral Triad

Yesod/Foundation (Sacral Center)

World of Manifestation

Malkuth/Kingdom (Root Center)

Base of Spine

Middle-Pillar Energy-Path, Centers and Sephiroth

through the agency of God's Word, the Christ, in the Spiritual/Moral Triad, activating creation's universal energy field in Yesod where, to quote Albert Einstein, "the field is the sole governing agency of the particle" ("the particle" here being the innumerable vibrating energy-wave elementary particles that are the hidden basis of all the atoms in the physical Universe). We'll have more to say about this in the following chapter.

Yesod is also a governing agency, but not the sole one, for the manifestation of human consciousness in the Personality/Astral Triad; Tiphareth, the Son, being the other, higher governing agency. So Yesod, under Tiphareth, contains the master pattern for the manifestation and evolution of all matter, life and consciousness in the physical Universe. Yesod's foundational patterns, created by Natural Law in us and by our limited free will, also govern the activities of our human personalities in the nonphysical realms of the Personality/Astral Triad.

As "the sphere of the activity of the union of Divine Father and Divine Mother," Yesod is the astral nexus of our soul's sexual or reproductive energies. Yesod holds the reproductive organs of "Adam Kadmon," the "Grand Man" or "Cosmic Self," who, in Qabalah, is where the Tree of Life corresponds to the inner structure of the Universe and to the physical body of the human microcosm. Our reproductive organs in Yesod pertain not only to physical reproduction, but also to the subconscious mind's automatic reproduction of all habit-patterns of thought, emotion, speech, desire and action that express our personality.

Our human personality's inner structure is lodged in Yesod, as our automatic habit-patterns of thought, feeling, speech and action. These habit-patterns include our instinctual needs and their distortions into emotional programs for happiness. We do not have to think about these habit-patterns consciously. They arise spontaneously from our subconscious as automatic responses or reactions to the people, places and things we encounter in daily life. These automatic habit-patterns express our personality and reveal its positive and negative programming. We are the inheritors and creators of this automatic subconscious programming, which began with our life in human ground.

VI

Another Qabalistic name for Yesod/Foundation is "the automatic consciousness." This refers to Yesod's automatic responses and reproduction of various patterns it contains when we encounter inner and outer symbolic stimuli that activate them. The habitual, automatic aspects of the other Sephiroth in human ground that connect to Yesod (Hod, Netzach and Malkuth) are all housed in the subconscious depths of Yesod/Foundation. It is the foundation for all our patterns, all that we think, feel or do repeatedly. Yesod is the astral womb of all patterns that precede manifestation in our consciousness and in the outer world of Malkuth. It is a vast domain of many levels that collectively reflect the wide variety of expressions that may manifest in the Personality/Astral Triad, as human and sub-human consciousness, in our individual and Collective Unconscious, and in the outer Universe. All of our thoughts and emotions impact the activity in Yesod, both in our self and in the collective Sphere of shared consciousness.

Yesod is the place in us where deep connections need to be made in order to change our daily-life consciousness and personality expression. As mentioned above, there is, on the Middle Pillar, an energy path running directly from Tiphareth down into Yesod. It's via this energy path that the divine action of Christ accesses Yesod to bring about purification, healing and change in the soul's unconscious energy field, where the hidden hard-drive patterns of the false self's emotional programming are lodged. It's here, in secret, where the essential spiritual work of contemplation and the divine therapy takes place in our soul. We'll have more to say about this most important and mysterious process in later chapters.

Yesod contains both our personal unconscious and the Collective Unconscious, made famous by the great Swiss psychologist, Carl Jung. The central archetype in Jung's map of the Collective Unconscious is called "the Self," meaning our true self.[2] Jung's "Self" correlates to Tiphareth, the Christ, on the Qabalistic Tree of Life and is accessed via deep silent meditation and contemplative prayer through a secret inner door in Yesod that opens into the energy path leading from Yesod up to Tiphareth in the Spiritual/Moral Triad. In order for this door to open, there needs to be inner peace and absolute calm in the subconscious or "animal-soul" area of Yesod. This is the path that leads to inner transformation and rebirth in Christ.

Most of the archetypes in Jung's Collective Unconscious are derived from the evolutionary history of humanity and life on Earth. This living historical material (the Archetypes of the Collective Unconscious) is appropriately stored in the soul's Yesod/Foundation, where all memories, patterns and impressions of life on Earth are held. Jung's spiritual archetype of the Self, however, is not a memory from our past evolution but the calling herald of our future evolution into integral wholeness and spiritual awakening in Christ, what Jung called "the individuation process." So Jung's "Self," which we may call our "true self" or "divine indwelling," resides in the higher, deeper central realm of the human soul, as Tiphareth or Christ, the Son of God, in the Spiritual/Moral Triad.

One of the deeper, older layers of Jung's Collective Unconscious is what Qabalah calls the "animal soul," mentioned earlier. This vital, animal soul in Yesod corresponds to the subconscious mind and is shared in common among humans, animals and all life on Earth. It has also been called the "Anima Mundi" or "World Soul." The vital, animal soul is a level of instinctive telepathic connection and psychic experience shared subconsciously and, in some cases, consciously among living organisms via the primitive language of subjective feelings, impulses and pictorial mental images. Some aboriginal humans still have conscious access to this "animal-soul" level of Yesod. It plays a central role in primitive magic, shamanism and animistic Nature worship.

Instinctive fear, sexual behavior, aggression and the universal "fight or flight" response are typical examples of the animal soul in operation among humans and in lesser evolved species. Its motivational driving force is the unwritten language of biological instinct, survival and the "subconscious group-mind," which is another name for the animal soul in Yesod. This primitive "group-mind" or herd instinct precedes the evolution of individual consciousness on the physical level, which develops by degrees among higher evolved species and in humans.

We share certain basic instinctual needs, drives and passions with animals through the animal soul in Yesod. This is where our instinctual tendencies toward kindness and cruelty first evolved. Since our innate tendencies toward kindness and cruelty are the terrestrial antecedents of good and evil in human nature, the animal soul in us has a dark, ominous side to it, and is the essential precursor to human free will on the moral/ethical level. The subconscious mind or automatic consciousness of the animal soul does not distinguish or judge between right and wrong or good and evil because it is innocent of the knowledge of good and evil, which dawns at a higher level of evolution in the self-reflective conscious mind and intellect of Hod. At most, our pre-rational subconscious mind or animal soul responds to its pre-programmed or learned attractions and aversions or likes and dislikes.

Since the subconscious animal soul is essentially driven by instinct and accepts without question whatever is put into it, it's subject to programming, manipulation and control by repeated positive or negative input that may come from outside influences or from within us. This programming is called "conditioning" in Western behavioral psychology. What's called a "conditioned response" involves the subconscious association of one stimulus with another, so that the presentation of the first stimulus will automatically elicit a response to both the presented stimulus and the one subconsciously associated with it, as in the famous case of "Pavlov's Dog." [3] Some common examples of humans being conditioned to respond automatically in thought, feeling and action come from commercial advertising, political propaganda, hypnotic suggestion and cultural conditioning. Being conditioned with various habits and responses to stimuli is part of how humans function. The conditioning we receive may be beneficial or detrimental to our wellbeing, freedom and spiritual growth.

Consequently, our subconscious mind may function as an adversary or an ally, depending on its programming and our continuing development of habit-patterns of thought, feeling, speech, belief, desire and action. Some examples of conflicting habit-patterns programmed into the subconscious may be as follows: emotional programs for happiness; moral/ethical integrity; likes and dislikes based on what's really good for us versus false appetites and desires; beliefs we acquire from self-knowledge, cultural/religious conditioning, advertising, peer pressure and misinformation. All of this affects our health and wellbeing. Three personal practices to help counter negative subconscious programming and inner conflicts are: 1) cultivating moral/ethical integrity, 2) speaking, knowing and acting on the truth, and 3) turning our subconscious and unconscious into friends and allies by acknowledging, respecting and paying close attention to them.

Honestly seeing and lovingly accepting our self and others as we are, combined with consistently listening to and following our conscience, serves to move us in the direction of positive, healthy self-programming. This is essential for doing our part in cooperating with the divine action in our soul. Transforming unhealthy subconscious patterns in Yesod is the nub of the battle to overcome evil tendencies and the false-self system. This wonderful inner work of redemption is accomplished in us by Christ, the Son (Tiphareth), who is always working to pour the spiritual gold of divine light, life and love into our soul's human ground. The goal of this inner work is to manifest the divine-image pattern of what we're intended by God, the Father, to become. This work requires our conscious consent and willing cooperation on all levels. Regular periods of daily Centering Prayer (or other receptive contemplative practice), living a life grounded in gospel values, and consenting to the divine action in us are ways we may facilitate this liberating healing process which leads to rebirth in Christ.

Rebirth in Christ moves us into higher levels of religious expression and experience where, by God's grace, we learn to live daily life consciously in God's presence. Differing levels of religious expression and experience correspond to different Sephiroth of the Personality/ Astral and Spiritual/Moral Triads. For example, the earliest, most primitive religions began on the level of Yesod with animistic Nature worship, sacrificial rituals and the animal soul; more conscious conceptual and intellectual aspects of religion evolved in Hod; and religion's emotional, devotional expressions arose in Netzach; as they all do today.

All religious expressions and experiences confined to the Personality/Astral Triad are grounded in either subconsciousness (Yesod) or separate-self consciousness (Hod and Netzach) and all tend to relate to their gods or God as an external Being or beings outside the self. As religious expression and experience evolve up into the Spiritual/Moral Triad, one discovers a connection to inner guidance and the true self in Tiphareth. A new dimension of spiritual life and relation to God emerges from this. We gradually realize we're not separate from God or the divine presence but part of a mysterious

Universal Consciousness. This realization awakens a radically new perspective that goes beyond the separate-ego into an awareness of co-participation in ongoing creation and the life of the Spirit.

Assuming any perspective of separate-self consciousness as the absolute basis of reality creates divisions and limits how God and spirituality are interpreted; that is, within a dualistic framework. Religious interpretations, practices and experiences limited to the Personality/Astral Triad versus those that integrate the Personality/Astral with the Spiritual/Moral Triad are two very different categories of personal spiritual life, each with its own purpose and validity. Appreciating and respecting these differences is one way of understanding the difference between exoteric (outer or dualistic) and esoteric (inner or mystical) spirituality and religion.

6

MALKUTH/KINGDOM AND DAATH/THE CLOUD

I

Malkuth/Kingdom, the tenth Sephira, is the Sphere of the human personality's outer expression in this world. This includes our physical body and senses (through which we contact our environment), as well as our consciousness in the human brain and nervous system. Malkuth is the end product or "fruit" on the Tree of Life. It's also the starting point and arena for our soul's spiritual evolution and conscious journey of return whence it came into being in created reality. As the soul evolves up the Tree in the human ground of Malkuth, the fruit on the Tree of Life gradually ripens toward fulfillment of God's plan, which is to share and express the most wonderful wealth and goodness, the love, truth and freedom of non-created Reality in all that God has created.

Our physical organism in Malkuth is a most precious possession, affording us opportunities to evolve through various experiences and relationships. This evolution involves moral/ethical choices and how we use our abilities to create change in our self, our consciousness and our environment. The vital energy or "etheric body" that animates our physical body in Malkuth is a function of the animal soul in Yesod and its formative energy field that organizes the structure and movement of physical matter. The Middle-Pillar energy path connecting Yesod and Malkuth is the passageway for the vital energy that animates our physical body.

The patterns of our animal nature's basic instinctual needs, which are lodged in Yesod, move down into Malkuth through the energy-channel connecting them and imprint themselves into our physical brain and body. There's a direct connection through this energy-channel between Yesod and the Central Nervous System, as there is between the chakras or subtle energy centers of the etheric body and the endocrine glands in our physical organism, e.g., the pineal, pituitary and thyroid glands. Hod and Netzach in the Personality/Astral Triad also have energy paths leading down into Malkuth through which our thoughts, images and emotions directly influence the cells, nerves, organs and biochemistry in the physical body. The connections between Malkuth and the Personality/Astral Triad are the basis of psychosomatic health and illness where thoughts, feelings and patterns in the Personality/Astral Triad directly affect the conditions and energy in the physical body, and vice versa. It's a two-way, reciprocal relationship and energy exchange between soma and psyche where the physical and the metaphysical are in continual interaction, both consciously and unconsciously.[1] Malkuth and the three Spheres above it are all involved in this process which creates life in human ground.

Reverence for life and God's creation is an important aspect of human spirituality. We may find God's presence in Nature and the healthy gratification of our basic needs for security/survival/safety, sensation/pleasure, affection/esteem/approval, power/control and intimacy/belonging. Our physical body in Malkuth is a temple of the Holy Spirit and dwelling place of the divine image, and deserves to be reverenced as such (1 Cor. 6:19–20). Consequently, our life in human ground is meant to be enjoyed, celebrated and appreciated; to love life, affirm its goodness and the beauty of creation is true prayer and worship. At the same time, the instincts, passions and appetites of our animal nature need to be tamed, moderated and balanced, if we're to appreciate and enjoy the good things in life as doors to God's presence.

Malkuth is the place of human relationships which are energy exchanges where we may share, learn from and enrich one another in various ways. We are challenged here to live the gospel values of love, forgiveness, honesty and kindness in Malkuth's arena of opportunities for spiritual growth and consciousness evolution. Our thoughts and emotions affect others and the environment around us, as well as within us. This happens individually within the soul and collectively through the group mind. How humans shape their physical environment is an expression of their consciousness evolution. We are responsible for care of the Earth and its ability to support life forms in harmony with Nature and God's plan. Caring for the Earth or spoiling it is part of the dramatic struggle between good and evil (saying "Yes" or "No" to life) in Malkuth/Kingdom. Our thoughts and desires in Hod and Netzach as well as the patterns and shadows in Yesod have direct impacts on the struggle of life against death in our midst. What then of evil and its destiny?

In English, *evil* is the word *live* spelled backward. This linguistic fact reveals something basic about evil and its destiny. According to Qabalistic teaching, there's an energy vortex in creation's lower recesses beneath Malkuth where all structures of will, desire and consciousness that are incapable of following the divine plan and evolving up the Tree are broken down and disintegrated. This vortex is a hellish place of disharmony, negativity and ultimate unconsciousness. It's the lower abyss of destruction that is the ultimate fate and goal of the path of evil, which seeks return to non-created Reality by way of saying "No" to existence and "No" to God's plan. Such total rebellion and rejection of God's loving will for us cannot be done by any soul or consciousness that's connected to the Spiritual/Moral Triad, where God lives in us as our true self or divine image in Tiphareth/Christ.

The traditional Qabalistic name for this negative energy-vortex and lower abyss on the Tree beneath Malkuth is "the Qlippoth,"[2] also called "Sheol," "the netherworld" and "the Pit" in Psalm 30:3. It's like creation's waste can or recycling bin where whatever refuses or is unable to evolve in a positive way, because of alienation or severance from the divine indwelling in the Spiritual/Moral Triad, is returned to non-created Reality via disintegration, death and destruction, i.e., unconsciousness. Such split-off conscious entities or dark demons of perversion and evil are similar to what Carl Jung referred to as "autonomous complexes" that take on a separate life of their own within the psyche or, in terms of the Tree of Life, within the Personality/Astral Triad in separation from the Spiritual/Moral Triad.

Such conscious pathological thought forms and demonic entities have been created within the soul not by God but by unevolved humans from the earliest times. Some of these collective thought forms have been worshipped as pagan gods, fierce guardians, horrible destroyers and powerful nature-spirits that became awesome archetypes in the primitive psyche and Collective Unconscious of Yesod/Foundation. These relatively independent entities are actually creations of the darkest human imaginings, animal passions and desires fed by superstitious beliefs, bloody sacrifices and human energy from time immemorial. These dark entities are demonic parasites of our making that live secretly in individual souls and in the darker regions of the collective astral world of the Personality/Astral Triad, especially in the shadowy netherworld of Yesod.

Such thought forms feed on human energy and come from savage passions, afflictive emotions and disowned shadow aspects of the false self, rejected aspects of the soul that incline toward evil. Like failed experiments, they are humanly created monsters that can't be integrated into the evolving soul's spiritual light. They hide in the shadows of the Personality/Astral Triad and will eventually be eliminated as the true spiritual light from above dissipates their hiding places and forces them to retreat into the darkness below, into the lower recesses of the Qlippoth's outer darkness beneath Malkuth. While they persist, they live off the soul's life-force energy and the energy of others. These autonomous shades of the dark side are liable to spread their toxic contagions of fear, lust, greed, hatred, violence, cruelty and perversion, causing great harm to self and others. The "Qlippoth" or negative recycling bin beneath Malkuth (the physical Universe) is the appropriate place for their gradual disintegration, destruction and unconscious return to non-created Reality.

II

According to Qabalistic teachings, Malkuth/Kingdom is made up of the four classic elements of ancient philosophy: Earth, Water, Air and

Fire. These elements are also active in the Personality/Astral Triad. Earth is the physical body itself; Water is the emotions, desire and liquids within the body; Air is the intellect and gases in the body; and Fire is the instinctual sex drive, passions, and heat created by the body's activities and temperature. These elements are harmonized on the energy path leading up from Malkuth into Yesod. The Christ or divine indwelling in Tiphareth balances the elements in the personality so they may cooperate together for spiritual growth and consciousness evolution; and these in turn, through the energy paths connecting the Personality/Astral Triad to Malkuth, balance the four elements in Malkuth, so the physical body may enjoy harmonious functioning and good health.

Our physical body and the various material objects in Malkuth seem to be quite solid; at least this is what our physical senses tell us. We can see movement in the four elements, in the changes of life, death and the weather, in the annual cycle of seasons, and in the heavenly bodies above; but we cannot see all the movement and activity going on within our own bodies and in the solid objects around us. According to Qabalistic, Tree-of-Life teaching, there's a continual movement of whirling energy on the hidden elementary level, where Yesod's patterns for outer manifestation in Malkuth take expression through a universal energy field underlying all physical manifestation in the Universe. This energy field is the pathway on the Tree connecting Yesod to Malkuth on the universal, macrocosmic level.

There is, on the hidden elementary level, an underlying consciousness or spiritual force connecting Yesod and its patterns to Malkuth and governing the out-manifesting activity of creation in the three-dimensional Universe at the bottom of the Tree. This underlying, root consciousness comes from Kether in the Supernal Triad, where the whirling of creation's energy begins, and where the image of the divine plan is held in God's omnipresent consciousness through the activity of the union of Divine Father (Chokmah) and Divine Mother (Binah), which takes place in the Sphere of Yesod, the Sephira of created reality's patterns for expression in Malkuth and the Personality/Astral Triad.

Modern science has corroborated the older Qabalistic teaching that, on a deep interior level, physical objects in Malkuth are not as solid and fixed as they outwardly appear to be. The objective investigation of Malkuth is the province of the physical sciences, e.g., physics, astronomy, chemistry, geology and biology. What we call "science" today began with the four classic elements of ancient philosophy and the idea of the atom as the basic, irreducible building block of physical matter. A little history may bring us up to date:

Sir Issac Newton (1642–1727) was an English philosopher and mathematician who, among other things, formulated the law of gravitation. With his calculations, Newton was able to chart the movements of the planets in our Solar System. In Newtonian physics, physical matter is primary and the atom (spoken of by ancient Greek philosophers) is assumed to be the smallest unit of matter out of which everything else is made. Newton was reasoning brilliantly on the basis of outward appearances but God was left out of the equation, due in part to apparently irreconcilable differences between scientific discoveries and older, rigid dogmas of the Church—like the Earth being the center of the Universe around which the heavens revolve. Many important discoveries of Western Science and our common sense understanding of how things work in the physical world are based on Newtonian physics.

By the end of the Nineteenth Century, physicists building on Newton's ideas believed they'd discovered all the laws of physics that operate in the Universe. They believed all that remained to be done was simply to classify everything and apply their knowledge to the various physical sciences in order to learn all there is to know about the world. However, around this time, some dramatic new discoveries were made that first challenged and then disproved the idea that Newtonian physics was the final word on the laws operating in the Universe. Radiation, x-rays and the electron were discovered, Max Planck developed the quantum hypothesis pertaining to the emission of invisible energy waves, and Albert Einstein began formulating his famous Theory of Relativity.

Newtonian physics views the Universe and human body as machines that operate according to set mechanical laws that are grounded in solid physical matter, the atom being the smallest unit of matter. The discovery of the electron disproved the assumption that atoms are either solid or the smallest unit of creation. Atoms were found to be composed of smaller elementary particles with positive, negative and neutral charges—i.e., protons, electrons and neutrons. The discovery of invisible energy-waves, e.g., X-rays, further disproved the absolute solidity of atoms and physical matter. Science had come upon some of the deeper mysteries of Malkuth, mysteries hidden from our gross physical senses.

These discoveries began a revolution in scientific thinking regarding creation, matter and the laws of physics. This revolution, which continues today, led to Einstein's general and special theories of relativity and the birth of quantum mechanics in 1925, along with Heisenberg's "uncertainty principle" as an integral part of it. The uncertainty principle states that it's not possible to determine the location and speed of an electron at the same time. A continuing stream of new theory, research and discoveries has issued forth from the fertile fountain of quantum mechanics, which subsumed Newtonian physics into itself and became the radical new foundation of physics.

Of special significance for understanding the reality underlying Malkuth/Kingdom are Einstein's Unified Field Theory (which attempts to integrate all the findings of physics) and something less widely known of from quantum mechanics called "the Zero Point Field." Quantum mechanics have revealed that energy underlies matter. Atoms are not solid, as previously believed. Instead, they are vortices of whirling energy containing tiny miniature tornadoes of subatomic particles emitting force fields that are in constant interaction; this is not unlike how the Sephiroth on the Tree of Life operate, from Kether/Crown, where the whirling of creation's energy begins on the most universal level, down into Malkuth, where it continues on the tiniest quantum level. The subatomic particles in atoms are simultaneously particles and waves that send out and receive quanta of light (photons) in their interactions with each other and in the interactions among atoms. Though proven scientifically, this basic information and its implications are yet to be integrated into our consensus view of reality, and may seem like a perplexing Zen koan or paradox confronting our conventional ways of thinking. From here, it goes even further:

What gives physical matter its apparent solidity and the characteristics perceived by our senses (which are also made up of whirling elementary particles and atoms generating force fields) is not any solidity inherent to the matter itself. It's the resistance created by the collective force fields generated by the spinning elementary particles within the atoms that creates our impressions or experiences of relative solidity and other specific characteristics of physical objects. This conceptual conundrum and experiential paradox is obviously some elaborate trick of Nature played as the divine consciousness manifests Malkuth and the energy field of created reality into our consciousness.

When the force fields generated by the atoms of our physical senses (in our physical bodies) bump up against the force fields of the various physical objects we contact (solid, liquid, radiating or gaseous), this creates our varied experiences of solidity and other characteristics, e.g., color, sound, temperature, smell, taste, shape, etc., of physical matter. One implication of this is that the phenomenal world we perceive is only relatively real in the ways we perceive and interpret it, like an extremely lucid dream. This notion is strikingly similar to some of the profounder mystical insights found in certain schools of the Eastern Religions, like those of Buddhism and Vedanta in Hinduism.

On the quantum level invisible to our senses, the qualities and characteristics of matter that we experience in Malkuth are actually non-material force fields of vibrating energy patterns pushing up against each other. There actually are no solid physical objects out there in the surrounding environment, or in the Universe at large, in the absolute sense of the word *solid*. It's the strength and power of the interacting force fields that gives physical matter its apparent or relatively real solidity. Ultimately, our perceived solidity of things is an illusion. This quantum insight is obviously a fine and subtle point that challenges our imagination (some may say our sanity!), while contradicting our culturally conditioned, consensus views of reality and experience. On the level of Newtonian physics, physical matter is solid and the laws of Newtonian physics are practical and real. The point here is that there's something more subtle and hidden from our sight that underlies this, something (if we choose to so interpret it) with profound metaphysical and spiritual implications.

What are these implications? It's now known that everything in the Universe is made up of energy that, according to Einstein's Unified Field Theory and the Zero Point Field discovery, exists in one unified, interactive energy field governed by a set of universal laws. In one of his wonderfully succinct quotes, Einstein says, "The field is the sole governing agency of the particle." The particle (which is both particle and wave) is what constitutes physical matter. The field is the non-physical, invisible energy field within, around and containing physical matter. What Einstein seems to be saying is that what happens in the energy field (Yesod on the Tree of Life) is what forms, shapes and determines what matter does and becomes. The field being the sole governing agency of the particle has further implications pertaining to mind and consciousness, which are also parts of the greater field described by the Tree of Life.

As reported by Lynne McTaggart in her popular book, *The Field*, scientists have discovered there are a variety of interactions between our thoughts and the energy field of created reality. Some of these interactions defy our conventional Newtonian views of the limits of time and space. Our thoughts, and all levels of our soul, interact and are contained within the great energy field of created reality (symbolized by the Tree of Life) and are connected to God or non-created Reality. Since, from a mystical perspective, created reality exists and is happening within God's consciousness, it seems obvious that it's God's thoughts and will that are guiding the universal energy field of created reality and the processes within it; but in a way that allows us free will and which only God fully knows or understands. When Einstein was asked if he agreed with those quantum physics scientists who said that what happens in the Universe happens randomly, his answer reportedly was, "God does not play dice with the Universe."

The fact that physical matter has no inherent solidity, as proven by quantum mechanics, is analogous to the fact, revealed by spiritual intuition and higher consciousness, that our ego or separate-self sense (false self) possesses no inherent substantiality, solidity or enduring reality. What quantum mechanics has discovered regarding the insubstantiality of phenomena through scientific experimentation, human consciousness may discover through deep introspection, silent meditation and contemplative prayer. What human consciousness may encounter in the silent depths of the soul, where no time, place or thing exists, corresponds to what quantum physicists have called "the Zero point Field," the "zero point" being that place at the ultimate center or bottom of things where an infinitely small point embraces and contains the infinitely large totality of created reality's universal energy field. This zero point is the point of mystical transcendence of all categories and concepts, similar to the invisible dark Sephira, Daath/the Cloud.

Physicists have known about the Zero Point Field since 1925. Yet they have disregarded it and kept it out of their equations, so that their calculations could work and wouldn't go on to infinity. Officially, they've tried to limit the Zero Point Field to inorganic matter and the subatomic level of created reality. As Bruce Lipton suggests,[3] an additional reason for this may be that fully acknowledging the Zero Point Field would have revolutionary implications for our culturally conditioned, consensus views of physical reality, i.e., its solidity, and our habitual customary views of our separate-selves as possessing inherent ego-solidity.

We perceive things and ourselves as being separated in time and space. This is fundamental to our separate-self consciousness. The Zero Point Field reveals everything to be interconnected in an underlying unity that transcends time and space in such a way that, on the innermost quantum level, all things interpenetrate one-another and we are all One. This, of course, is a spiritual interpretation of the Zero Point Field where everything co-exists and vibrates together in a mysterious inner dimension beyond the separations of time, space and substance. This supports the fundamental thesis of mystical spirituality and consciousness. The spiritual implication of the Zero Point Field is that there is no absolute separate-self identity for any of us in the final analysis. We are all part of the One Divine Consciousness of Kether and the Limitless Light within which exist the great Tree of Life and all that it manifests. This insight, if taken seriously, is a highly radical and revolutionary realization from the perspectives of our false self, cultural conditioning and separate-self sense.

The above is, again, a mystical/spiritual interpretation of the Zero Point Field and the findings of quantum mechanics. I don't think it could be proven by any scientific experiments and I doubt most physicists would agree with it. It's an extrapolation from the known to the unknown and from the proven to the unproven, in terms of physical scientific evidence. It undermines worldly common sense and our culturally conditioned ideas of "normal" reality, to which physicists are generally quite attached, along with the rest of us.

With the Zero Point Field, or at least the above mystical interpretation of it, the implications of scientific discovery have come full circle to reach the central point or essence of what's meant by the word *religion*, the Latin origin of which, *religare*, means "to bind back to origins." Zero Point is obviously the origin, "the circle whose center is everywhere and whose circumference is nowhere"—to quote St. Augustine. With this in mind, we might say that God's Divine Consciousness is the ultimate Zero Point Field.

III

The Zero Point Field is not an abyss but a point of paradoxical transcendence that exits the realm of duality and the play of opposites in created reality by opening into the underlying, omnipresent universal energy field out of which created reality emerges, not only on the physical level of Malkuth, but on all levels of created reality throughout the Tree. On the spiritual level, the Zero Point Field equates to St. Augustine's famous description of God as a circle whose center is omnipresent. As a hidden metaphysical symbol of spiritual reality, perhaps the Zero Point Field tells us something about the mystery of God's hidden omnipresence? The timeless, paradoxical concept of the Zero Point Field points in the direction of Daath/the Cloud and the higher abyss of unconsciousness and non-conceptual contemplative prayer in which the individual soul is brought by God through the walls of separation in time and space into the ineffable light, life and love of universal consciousness in the Supernal Triad.

There are two abysses on the Tree of Life that lead from created reality into non-created Reality. These two abysses correspond to the spiritual paths of good and evil. Daath/the Cloud is associated with the higher abyss of apophatic contemplation that leads the soul into rebirth in Christ and the fullness of conscious participation in the divine light, life and love of non-created Reality. The lower abyss, below Malkuth, is created reality's waste can or recycling bin, mentioned earlier and known in Qabalah as the "Qlippoth." What are drawn into the Qlippoth are our errors—our faulty creations—not God's. Created in the divine image, we have relative free will and the power to create, in thought, word, wish and deed; and we're responsible for what we create and its impacts on others. When our creations take on a life of their own apart from our conscious will, we're still responsible for them.

Physical and nonphysical reality both exist on one great continuum of energy-wave vibrations within the divine consciousness of God (Supernal Triad and Limitless Light). Just as nonphysical energy-patterns from Yesod and the Zero Point Field may coalesce into physical substance, so may physical matter be broken down or disintegrated into unstructured energy, as in radical dismemberment or an explosion. The same holds true for patterns and structures of thought, feeling and consciousness in the astral matter of the Personality/Astral Triad. That is, whatever is composed of nonphysical astral matter in realms invisible to our physical senses may also be broken down and disintegrated into unstructured energy and dissipated consciousness. This is actually part of our soul's interior purification process under the divine action; and it's what happens to created reality's waste products of irredeemable, hard core evil in the lower abyss or negative energy vortex of disintegration and death under Malkuth, which empties its contents back into non-created Reality as unconscious raw primal energy. This process is analogous to how the human body eliminates its waste products.

Symbolized by an inverted triangle, the Qlippoth or lower abyss is the ultimate "black hole" of non-existence to which evil ultimately aspires (knowingly or unknowingly). It's the "Pit" or void of nothingness at the absolute bottom of the Tree of Life, the outer darkness whence nothing returns. Entering the Qlippoth is the consequence of saying "No" to existence and God's plan, of preferring cruelty, perversion and destruction instead. Hence, the lower abyss of disintegration is the extreme opposite of Tiphareth, the soul's integral center, and of the absolute unity, pure consciousness and fulfillment of Kether, at the top of the Tree. Only demonic entities or pathological split-off complexes that are not connected to Christ and the divine image, and that are useless for evolution, are drawn into the Qlippoth. The Lord destroys not his own image. Perhaps, the Qlippoth is the "furnace of fire, where there will be weeping and gnashing of teeth," Jesus mentions in Matthew 13:42; that is, the place of destruction for the weeds in our soul (Matt. 13:24–30). The Qlippoth in Qabalah may also be identified with "Gehenna," "the hell of fire" and "place of destruction" Jesus speaks of in Matthew 18:9 and 7:13–14.

The divine image in the soul's true center is the basis of its immortality. Apart from its divine indwelling, the personality or false self has no substantial inner being and cannot endure beyond the space of a lifetime. The Lord destroys not his own holy image, even in souls who betray their conscience. Such souls are bound to the consequences and expiation of their errors on the road of suffering, service and disillusionment, until their integrity is restored through inner purification, healing and harmony with the Higher Self in Tiphareth, the Son. Yet, Severity (Geburah) is balanced by Mercy (Chesed), and forgiveness is available through the kindness and compassion of the Lord's patient love.

We have but to humbly acknowledge the truth of our soul, sincerely repent into a way of life that pleases the Lord, and our sins are forgiven freely and fully in the grace of God's mercy. In general, that which is divided and apart from the divine indwelling remains under the law of duality (Geburah/Severity), while that which becomes integrated and united in Christ attains to the mercy of love (Chesed/Mercy), the higher spiritual law of oneness and divine love that Jesus teaches us about.

The prodigal soul is welcomed home in the embrace of God's love (Luke 15:11–32). This teaching of forgiveness is part of the wonderful "good news" Jesus came to proclaim, if we can believe it. It marks the radical transition from the dualistic justice of "an eye for an eye and a tooth for a tooth" (Geburah/Severity) into the unitive justice of God's magnanimous generosity under the higher spiritual law of universal love (Chesed/Mercy), which Jesus brought into the world. Jesus' entire life and his sacrificial death on the cross demonstrate this higher law of love and justice, which transcends dualistic concepts. Different interpretations of Cosmic Spiritual Law apply at different levels of consciousness on the Tree of Life—in Malkuth, the Personality/Astral Triad and Geburah/Severity dualistic interpretations apply, whereas in Chesed/Mercy, the pure love of Christ in Tiphareth and the Supernal Triad, dualistic interpretations are utterly transcended, and unitive interpretations of oneness apply.

In contrast to the Qlippoth, the lower abyss of disintegration at the bottom of the Tree, the higher abyss associated with Daath/the Cloud leads to the soul's integration into Christ and the Supernal Triad. Integration of the soul's masculine and feminine energies is the way to its evolution into wholeness, unity and higher consciousness. This creative integration of each soul and center of consciousness into increasingly higher levels of synthesis, unity and awareness in the love of Christ is the way of God's divine plan. This harmonious integration is symbolized by the union of Divine Father and Divine Mother in the Supernal Triad and is facilitated by our growth in love as we are assimilated and liberated into the Mystical Body of Christ.

Daath/the Cloud is called the "invisible Sephira" because it can't be replicated by imagination or conceived by the intellect. Like pure contemplation, it is utterly apophatic or without images. It's more of a "passing through place" than an "abiding place" on the Tree of Life, like the ten visible Sephiroth. Daath is the Sephira of "crossing the abyss" between the Spiritual/Moral Triad and the Supernal Triad. When this great abyss is crossed over time in contemplative prayer, the darkness of the unconscious is eventually transformed into Cosmic Consciousness, which transforms the soul's individual consciousness into participation in universal consciousness.[4]

Crossing the abyss in the microcosmic Tree of Life (individual soul) is not the same as it is on the Macrocosm or Universal Tree. This is because, beginning in Malkuth/Kingdom, there are ten degrees of Daath/the Cloud through which the soul's individual consciousness or Tree must pass in its journey into the fullness and perfection of divine union in Kether on the Universal Tree. That is, in each of the ten visible Sephiroth on the Tree, there is contained a smaller Tree of Life which the individual consciousness or soul must "climb" in order to complete the lessons or grades of spiritual growth available in each Sephira. Hence, there are ten degrees of Daath through which the individual evolving soul must pass in its journey from Malkuth and the refinements of individual consciousness in the Personality/Astral and Spiritual/Moral Triads into the divine understanding (Binah), wisdom (Chokmah) and oneness (Kether) of universal consciousness in the Supernal Triad on the Universal Tree. This process represents the soul's "long journey home" or "journey of return" in Qabalah— symbolized in the "Prodigal Son" parable.

We cannot know Daath/the Cloud with our intellect, but only via firsthand experience. There's no other way to get a real feel for it. Like all the mysteries, trials and wonders of human and spiritual life that require direct personal experience, we may only talk about and around Daath, pointing toward it with concepts and symbols. Just as all our ideas of God must fall short of the reality because they're not God but only our creations pointing toward God, so is it with our ideas and images concerning Daath. Hence, they may fall upon paradox or appear inconsistent. We need to humbly remember that our human intellect or concrete mind in Hod is a limited instrument— though capable of inspiration from above.

Daath is the invisible of the invisible that may not be accurately represented by word or image, unlike the ten visible Sephiroth we see represented on the Tree. We may intuit a non-verbal, non-conceptual sense of Daath by reflecting on words and images that point toward it, e.g., "non-conceptual" and "the Cloud," and in "the laying aside of thoughts," as Evagrius of Pontus is said to have defined "prayer."[5] Hence, it's only in non-conceptual prayer or meditation that we may receive some actual sense of Daath by "sinking in" to the nondescript silence of "resting in God," as apophatic contemplation has been traditionally defined.

Our movement into some degree or level of Daath in Centering Prayer is movement into the silent space where the Divine Therapist goes to work in the unconscious recesses of our soul in Yesod in the Personality/Astral Triad to heal our hidden wounds and remove the obstacles that prevent us from living the gospel values and freely accessing our life in Christ (Tiphareth) and the divine presence. Resting in God in interior silence is resting in Daath/the Cloud. A cloud is something that changes shape, is vague and indistinct. Hence, it's an appropriate image for the invisible Sephira. We find the appearance of the cloud as a symbol of God's overshadowing presence in both the Old and New Testaments.

For example, in Exodus 24:16 we read, "The glory of the Lord settled on Mount Sinai, and the cloud covered it for six days; on the seventh day he called to Moses out of the cloud." Exodus 34:5 says, "The Lord descended in the cloud and stood with him there, and proclaimed the name, 'the Lord.'" This mysterious cloud of God's presence reappears in the New Testament at Jesus' transfiguration on Mount Tabor: "...a cloud came and overshadowed them; and they were terrified as they entered the cloud. Then from the cloud came a voice that said, 'This is my Son, my Chosen; listen to him!'" (Luke 9:34–35). Listening is the basic disposition of apophatic contemplative prayer.

In Exodus 33:14, God says to Moses, "My presence will go with you, and I will give you rest." This is a direct reference to the gift of contemplation or "resting in God." Fr. William Meninger, one of the founders of Centering Prayer, has said that Centering Prayer could have been called "the prayer of the Cloud," in reference to the anonymous, fourteenth century *Cloud of Unknowing* text.[6] So, God's mysterious presence and non-conceptual contemplative prayer are both associated with the symbol of the Cloud.

When, in Centering Prayer, we enter Daath/the Cloud in our individual soul's Yesod/Foundation through our physical-brain consciousness in Malkuth, this allows Tiphareth to descend the Middle Pillar into our unconscious to heal the wounds and work at removing the hidden obstacles embedded within us. This is the key inner work of Centering Prayer that, with our consent and cooperation, allows the Divine Therapist, i.e., Holy Spirit, divine indwelling or Christ, the Redeemer, to eventually purify, heal and transform our false-self personality expression into our true self or rebirth in Christ. This is the long-term aim of Centering Prayer evolving into a mature contemplative spirituality.

The "unloading of the unconscious," in which previously repressed material comes up and passes through our consciousness and physical body, is a basic sign that this important inner work is moving forward. Contrary to how it may feel or appear to us, unloading of the unconscious is actually a positive symptom of spiritual growth and progress in the uphill labor of freeing our soul from the thralldom and pain of the false self. This is the counterintuitive paradox of psycho-spiritual healing in the soul; that is, when we're actually getting better, it temporarily feels like we're getting worse. Tolerating and welcoming unloading the unconscious is an act of faith and trust in the Divine Therapist, as well as an act of surrender to God and the truth of our soul.

Submitting to the divine therapy is like entering a cloud of unknowing because we do not understand what is happening or why, and we are not in control of what's going on. We have to "let go and let God" in faith and trust. We are challenged to accept the truth of whatever comes up for us, especially when we don't like it because it's painful, frightening or makes us feel uncomfortable, uneasy, angry or sad. The intuitive notion of entering and traversing Daath/the Cloud suggests an appropriate ambience for "resting in God" in our contemplative journey through darkness and the unconscious into our life in Christ.

IV

In the continual interactions and energy exchanges among Malkuth, Yesod, Tiphareth and the other Sephiroth of the Personality/Astral, Spiritual/Moral and Supernal Triads, the Tree of Life glyph offers a clear, symbolic window or map for visualizing and understanding the mysterious workings of the mostly invisible process of our spiritual healing and renewal in Christ through Centering Prayer. The Tree is one map of created reality's invisible worlds and their workings. As such, it ought not to be taken too literally. It offers one way of understanding what we can't normally see.

The Tree is a visible representation of what's unseen but nonetheless real, a rolling out into separate details of something that's actually cohesive and integrated in itself, like the threads of a carpet woven to appear as many colors on the surface while remaining of one color underneath. Like the mystery of the Trinity, the Tree of Life and its Sephiroth are given us as a kataphatic representation of Ultimate Mystery that our minds may grasp, so we may advance in understanding God and God's creation. Beyond these visible representations are deeper, apophatic mysteries our hearts may embrace in love through the gift of contemplation. The revelation of these mysteries may come to us through the non-conceptual, invisible Sephira, Daath, which we may enter via the method of Centering Prayer and the deeper gift of contemplation.

One of these mysteries is the peaceful, loving divine consciousness that's within everything, like the one universal color within a many-colored carpet. We are invited, by God's grace, to participate in this divine universal consciousness that underlies, blesses and interpenetrates everything. It reveals God's patient love and concern for every soul, and this humble consciousness is, ultimately, our True Self.

Again, it's important to remember that the Tree of Life is not meant to be taken too literally. What I'm presenting here is my interpretation of the Tree and attempt to adapt some of its ancient teachings to the conceptual background of Centering Prayer—based on my limited knowledge of Qabalah, the Tree and how it may be used. There are other interpretations and applications I know little or nothing about.

In adapting the Tree of Life to the purposes of Centering Prayer and Christian Mysticism, some creative liberties—based on intuitive inspirations—have been taken, especially regarding Daath/the Cloud. I've done this in the spirit of Qabalah as "received" or "revealed teaching." On the following page is a summary diagram of the Tree of Life. In Part Two, we'll focus in more detail and depth on the inner transformation process of our evolution from false self to true self and rebirth in Christ.

Ain Soph Aur or Limitless Light

1

Kether/Crown · · · · · · · **Archetypal World**

Supernal Triad · · · · · · · **Universal Spiritual Ground**

3 · · · · · · · 2 · · · · · · · **Creative World**

Divine Mother · · · **Divine Father**

Binah/Understanding · · · Chokmah/Wisdom

5 · · · · · · · 4

Geburah/Severity · · · Chesed/Mercy

Spiritual/Moral Triad · · · · · · · **Individual Spiritual Ground**

6 · · · · · · · **Upper Formative World**

Tiphareth/Beauty

Christ, the Son

8 · · · · · · · 7

Hod/Splendor · · · Netzach/Victory

Personality/Astral Triad · · · · · · · **Human Ground**

9 · · · · · · · **Lower Formative World**

Yesod/Foundation

10

Malkuth/Kingdom · · · · · · · **World of Manifestation**

Qabalistic Tree of Life

PART TWO: REBIRTH IN CHRIST

7

Our Divine Inheritance

In the Qabalistic, allegorical interpretation of Genesis,[1] Adam and Eve are not seen as two separate human beings but as representing the self-consciousness (Adam) and subconsciousness (Eve) in all human beings. Also, as mentioned earlier, Adam represents generic humanity and Eve, as the Universal Mother (an expression of Binah/Understanding), is "the mother of *all* living" (Gen. 3:20). "All living" is understood to include every species of life form, not just human beings. In this Qabalistic interpretation, Adam and Eve take on universal, macrocosmic significance in addition to their roles as representing humanity in general and two basic components of each individual soul in particular, i.e., self-consciousness and subconsciousness.

Adam and Eve's epic journey down the Tree of Life, from their creation in the Supernal Triad to their entry into the "fallen state" of Malkuth/Kingdom, is the prototype for the creation and journey of each individual soul into human incarnation. The subsequent journey for each "fallen" soul is that of evolving back up the Tree through human ground into spiritual ground in the Spiritual/Moral Triad. This outlines our great journey from the soul's original Lost Paradise, down the Tree into Malkuth, up through human ground and into the new Paradise of our life in Christ. Each soul entering the new Paradise or "heavenly kingdom" will have developed its unique individuality and consciousness by evolving up through the Personality/Astral Triad and gaining wisdom in resolving the conflicts between good and evil within itself. Consequently, the soul's newly found Paradise in the Spiritual/Moral Triad will be dramatically different from the Paradise it left and lost as an infant soul. It will be something far superior

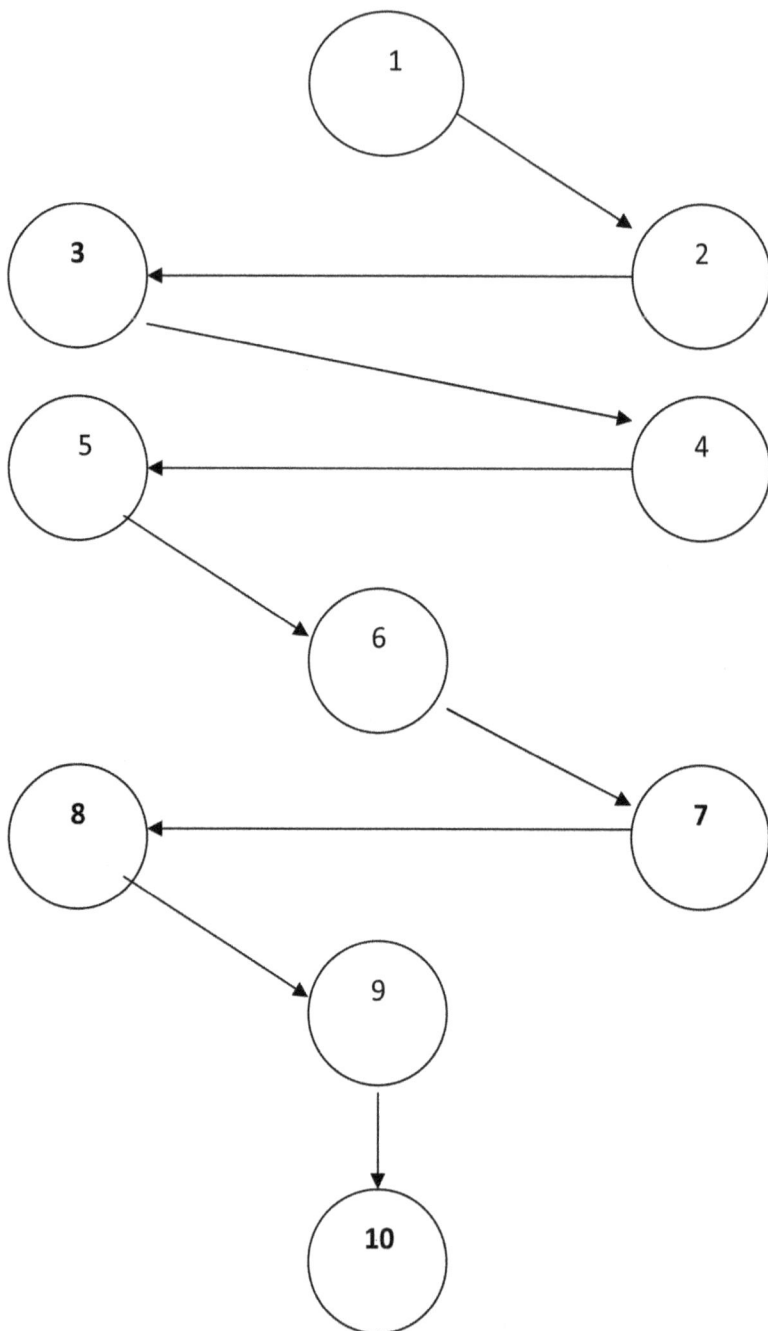

Movement of Energy and Images Down the Tree

to the peaceful rest and undifferentiated unity of its spiritual infancy and innocence.

The journey of Adam, Eve and each individual soul, from birth in Binah (Divine Mother, no. 3) down the Tree of Life into Malkuth, follows the lightning-flash pattern and path of the Sephiroth in numerical order (1 to 10) through the Three Sacred Triads and Four Qabalistic Worlds.[2] This process is initiated in Kether and the Archetypal World with the original inspiration or idea for creation and the divine plan. The plan's implementation begins in the World of Creation where God, as Divine Father and Divine Mother, creates the energy and images for the plan to take shape in the World of Formation (Spiritual/Moral and Personality/Astral Triads). The central players in this divine drama and great adventure are the living individual souls, represented by Adam and Eve, whose God-intended destiny is to evolve through created reality on the Tree of Life from relative unconsciousness into full consciousness and rebirth in Christ.

Primordial Adam/Eve is the prototype for all individual souls that eventually become human, once they've traveled down the Tree and are born internally divided into Malkuth and the "fallen" human condition of apparent separation from God. The primordial image of all souls (Adam) is formed in the Universal Womb of Binah and given its first-birth into individual spiritual ground, entering Chesed/Mercy in the uppermost region of the Spiritual/Moral Triad and World of Formation. Each newly born soul is a living, feeling energy field of unknowing innocence and purity, blind as a babe in its mother's womb. Transferred from Binah's Universal Womb across the Great Abyss into individual existence in Chesed, the infant soul experiences a timeless state of peace and harmony, intimacy and innocence, love and comfort. This is the place of our soul's Original Paradise, where Adam/Eve is one being, whole and complete in the holy womb of innocence and love.

It's a place of complete security, peace and bliss in the heart of spiritual ground where all is one in the pristine presence of divine love. There's nothing to desire here because the infant soul is content in the effortless fulfillment of all its immediate needs. The new soul feels whole and complete in itself as its deepest instinctual need for intimacy/belonging is fulfilled in divine love's warm embrace. The memory of this blessed experience, imprinted in its deepest center, is held in the soul's heart as it travels down the Tree and enters human embodiment. Adam and Eve, self-consciousness and subconsciousness, are one and the same in the dreamless sleep of absorption and rest in the precious nurturing love of timeless peace and effortless contentment. Each infant soul's sojourn in Chesed gives it the first imprint of our divine inheritance etched deep into its virgin core. It's a place of deep peace we all long to get back to.

The timeless state of blissful rest seems eternal, without beginning or end. Then a movement begins from within and without the timeless Paradise, drawing Adam/Eve (the infant individual soul) onto an undulating energy path across the Tree from the Pillar of Mercy to the Pillar of Severity, Mercy's polar opposite where divisions are drawn. Self-consciousness and subconsciousness are separated as the inner voice of creation's evolutionary impetus rises up in the soul, speaking to subconsciousness, urging change to the status quo and promise of something better to come. This inner voice is symbolized by the biblical Serpent in Genesis 3:1-5, addressing Eve, subconsciousness, beside the Tree of the Knowledge of Good and Evil where grows the "forbidden fruit," which bestows the power of the "discriminating intelligence," the second imprint of our divine inheritance.

Being innocent, naïve and susceptible to suggestion, subconsciousness (Eve) naturally complies and follows the Serpent's advice. "The rest," as they say, "is history." Something happens to the young, innocent soul in the holy sphere of Geburah, where its primal unity as enjoyed in Chesed is lost and subconsciousness and self-consciousness (Eve and Adam) are separated into an incomplete two rather than remaining as one, whole and complete as before in the Paradise of Chesed. Unlike what happens with the One and the Two in the Supernal Triad of Genesis One, the separation of one soul (represented by Adam and Eve) into two halves loses the consciousness of primal unity and falls under the spell of the Principle of Duality and the pairs of opposites. Hence, the soul is separated from its Original Paradise as Adam and Eve's "eyes.... were opened and they knew that they were naked" (Gen. 3:7).

In Geburah, the soul receives the fiery imprints of creation's life-force energy and its true spiritual conscience, the inner voice of divine guidance and wisdom it needs for negotiating the trials of good/evil choices and other challenges of life in human ground. The imprints of life-force energy and true conscience (knowledge of good and evil) are gifts of our divine inheritance held permanently in subconsciousness as intuitive desire, understanding and wisdom. The power of discrimination the soul receives from the "forbidden fruit" in the Sphere of Geburah is the basis for our free will in discerning and making choices. Discrimination allows consciousness to distinguish one thing from another and to perceive the pairs of opposites on various levels, e.g., physical, sensational, emotional, mental, moral/ethical, psychic, social and spiritual. The power of discrimination between "this" and "that" is the basis of our human separate-self ego-consciousness which, when made into an artificial absolute, creates our existential aloneness/incompleteness and false-self identity.

We need the wisdom of true conscience for guidance in relating to and using the creative power of life-force energy or Serpent-impulse within us. As experience teaches, the gifts bestowed by the "forbidden fruit" are empowering but also challenging and problematic. They release the untamed energy of the evolutionary Serpent-power and basic instinctual needs with which we are programmed and have to contend in pursuing freedom and spiritual growth. Possessing a conscience and knowledge of good and evil forces us to face moral/ethical challenges in how we live our lives, treat others, relate to God and go about pursuing our needs and desires.

Our struggles with egocentric self-centeredness and the life-force energy in our soul may serve to make us stronger and wiser as self-determining individuals. Successfully handling good/evil conflicts refines our character and brings us into harmony with conscience. Everything we face and contend with in human life, e.g., our false self and its emotional happiness programs, is part of the ingredients needed for the dramas of our personal and spiritual growth; and for the development of our individual character as a self-conscious entity and self-determining soul. In other words, the endowments of the "forbidden fruit" as part of our divine inheritance, and the challenges this brings, are essential for consciousness evolution, spiritual development and the unfolding of God's plan in us.

It's into the complexities of human existence that the biblical Serpent is urging Adam and Eve to venture when he/she induces them to eat the "forbidden fruit," saying, "You will not die; for God knows that when you eat of it your eyes will be opened, and you will be like God, knowing good and evil" (Gen. 3:4–5). The Serpent didn't lie with these words, but didn't tell the full truth either, i.e., what the consequences of eating the "forbidden fruit" would be. The consequences, i.e., the Fall and being subject to its fruits of 1) death/change; 2) sex/desire; 3) good/evil choices; and 4) aloneness/incompleteness apart from God, would be something that they, and each of us, would need to learn firsthand through real life experience in human ground.

Without the gifts bestowed by the "forbidden fruit," we would remain innocent, naïve and unable to cope with the challenges and issues of human life. We would not know the difference between right and wrong, which requires discriminating intelligence combined with awareness of basic ethics and morality beyond the immature viewpoints of childish or adolescent self-centeredness. Without the "forbidden fruit" and its gifts, the wisdom way to spiritual growth, which ironically restores our lost innocence, would not be open to us. From this perspective, it's clear that God's real intention or hidden agenda was for Adam and Eve to eat the "forbidden fruit," since God set the stage for both the Fall and God's plan for the evolution of human souls and consciousness into spiritual ground. This divine plan could not move forward unless Adam and Eve (we) did eat the "forbidden fruit" and subsequently develop individual free will, intelligence and consciousness.

In Chesed, the pure infant soul enjoys the sublime energy of divine love, quiet calm, peace and deep rest. In Geburah, on the opposite side of the Tree, the virgin soul is impacted by the driving energy of mental discrimination, moral/ethical sensitivity, motivation to action and the instinctual impulses of the restless Serpent-power within. Hence, the soul is programmed with the unity of love, the duality of discrimination and the hunger of desire. These contrasting experiences are the nascent seeds of the need to create balance between rest and activity, contemplation and action in our human life. From Geburah, the developing soul is drawn down into the third, central Sephira in the Spiritual/Moral Triad, Tiphareth/Beauty. In Tiphareth, the soul (Adam) receives the living imprint of Christ, the divine image, which is then stored in subconsciousness (Eve) as the latent program for the soul's future evolution from human consciousness into divine consciousness.

The living imprint of the divine image present in Tiphareth is the source of the soul's inner healing and growth when it progresses through the spiritual journey during its life in Malkuth. Our spiritual journey is a movement back up the Tree in reverse order of the Sephiroth (10 to 1). In Christ, the Son (Tiphareth), the soul's primal purity and innocence, its kindness, love and compassion (derived from Chesed), are restored and integrated with its knowledge of good/evil and its powers of creativity, discrimination and the values of conscience (received in Geburah). This transforming and liberating empowerment in the Central Sephira of the divine indwelling on the soul's return journey is the basis for finally harvesting our "forbidden fruit" of divine inheritance in the Spiritual/Moral Triad.

Tiphareth is the power of inner resurrection and renewal in the soul. This is not a power of the personality or separate-self sense, but of our deep inner self, true self, Higher Self or divine indwelling. This Sephira of the Central Self or Christ, the "anointed one" and Word of God, is the place of our soul's rebirth in Christ. It's the divine repository and transformer of all patterns, images and energies held in the soul. Christ is the one through whom new life, the Holy Spirit, is breathed into us by God, the "Father who sees in secret" of Matthew 6:6 (Chokmah). The Son in Tiphareth is the one through whom the Spiritual Sun awakens and shines in us as the overflowing fullness of divine love, truth and freedom, filling the soul that it may be fully born of water (purification), fire (illumination) and the Spirit (John 3:3-8). This is our rebirth in Christ, our soul's rebirth in its individual spiritual ground in the Spiritual/Moral Triad. In its return journey back up the Tree, the individual soul receives the fullness of its divine inheritance, an inner wealth of blessings and gifts as it harvests the now life-giving

Supernal Triad

(Universal Spiritual Ground)

1

Kether/Crown

3   **2**

Binah/Understanding   Chokmah/Wisdom

Spiritual/Moral Triad

(Individual Spiritual Ground)

5   **4**

Geburah/Severity   Chesed/Mercy

Tiphareth/Beauty

6

(Christ, the Son)

Personality/Astral Triad

(Human Ground)

8   **7**

Hod/Splendor   Netzach/Victory

9

Yesod/Foundation

10

Malkuth/Kingdom

Path of the Soul's Journey

"forbidden fruit" and becomes a unique expression of the divine image held in its deepest center.

In imprinting the souls of Adam (generic humanity) with his divine image, Christ becomes identified with humanity on the spiritual level. The difference between Christ, the Son of Man, and Adam, the archetypal "fallen" man, relative to the divine image is that in Christ (Tiphareth) the divine image is fully conscious, expressed and manifest; in Adam (humanity) this same divine image is generally unconscious, existing in subconsciousness as the latent potential of our as yet unrealized divine inheritance.

Fully coming into our divine inheritance by becoming the divine image within us, as Jesus did, is the primary goal of the spiritual journey and ultimate purpose of the divine plan. In his Last Supper Discourse, Jesus, the perfect human embodiment of Tiphareth (Christ, the Son), prays to God, the Father (Chokmah), that his disciples may come into the divine inheritance. He does this in John 17:22–23, where he prays to the Father on behalf of us all, "The glory that you have given me I have given them, so that they may be one as we are one, I in them and you in me, that they may become completely one." Thus, he speaks of our rebirth in Christ.

So, in Chesed, the soul receives the imprints and memory of rest in its Original Paradise. In Geburah, it receives the imprints of the divine life force, motivation to action, discrimination, knowledge of good/evil, and conscience. And in Tiphareth, the soul receives the living imprint of the divine image and plan for its evolution from human ground into spiritual ground (the heavenly New Jerusalem).

In Tiphareth, along with the divine image, the soul receives the creativity of integration and synthesis that empower it with the capacity for self-transformation and rebirth in Christ. This is the power of the divine indwelling to carry out God's plan for spiritual growth and consciousness evolution in the soul. It's a plan for the fulfillment of our divine inheritance as unique individual souls created in the divine image. We are all unique expressions of the universal divine image because the heredity, experiences, circumstances and relationships that form us in our physical and spiritual growth are all unique.

Thus does the divine Spiritual/Moral Triad on the Tree of Life imprint its treasures of living images and energies into the subconsciousness of each soul as it moves down the Tree to enter human ground in Malkuth through the doorway of the Personality/Astral Triad. In the Spiritual/Moral Triad (Chesed, Geburah and Tiphareth), Eve (subconsciousness) is impregnated with the patterns of the soul's evolutionary potentials (our divine inheritance), which are held latent within us awaiting development following our birth into human ground.

8

Unconscious Personality Patterns

I

If we possess a divine inheritance, why are we not able to freely access this inner treasure? The simple answer is there are obstacles in us that prevent us from doing so. In Romans 7:14–20, Paul expresses our lack of freedom and common dilemma: "I do not do what I want, but I do the very thing I hate." In human ground, we're caught in snares of the Personality/Astral Triad where conflicting desires of good and evil vie for dominion. Divided and trapped on this lower level, we're unable to access or claim our divine inheritance. Ironically, our blind attempts to do so often reinforce the false self.

The obstacles to freedom and growth in us are an inevitable consequence of the human condition into which we're born. One way of conceptualizing these inner obstacles is as unhealthy personality patterns. Unconscious personality patterns that are unhealthy keep us stuck at immature stages of development; that is, they keep us under the domination of childish attitudes and goals that are irrational, egocentric and out of sync with higher spiritual values. These patterns include each individual's false-self system and its emotional programs for happiness. As Thomas Keating teaches, the removal of our inner obstacles is the work of the divine therapy initiated by Centering Prayer. Such work, which may be carried out only on God's terms, requires our willing consent and cooperation. That is, it requires our trust in God's benevolence and wisdom, efforts to live true to conscience, and acceptance of the divine action—which works at times in ways we may not see or understand.

As with the soul's journey into human embodiment, the Qabalistic Tree of Life may be used to provide a visible map of our unconscious personality patterns, their origins, inner workings and transformation by Christ's healing action in the soul. These patterns are formed as a consequence of physical embodiment, early life experiences, and our subsequent reactions and choices. Prior to physical birth, the individual soul descends from Tiphareth into the Personality/Astral Triad, carrying the living imprints of divine inheritance received in the Spiritual/Moral Triad. This divine inheritance is our soul's inner treasure. The journey of creation's energy from Kether down into physical embodiment in Malkuth has been called "the fall of Spirit to matter." The fall of Spirit to matter is also the fall of God's divine consciousness into our relative unconsciousness in the three-dimensional Universe, whence the evolutionary journey of individual souls back up the Tree begins.

The soul receives its human inheritance in the Personality/Astral Triad. First are the imprints of Netzach/Victory, containing the seeds of our human emotions, desire nature, will and imagination. Next, in Hod/Splendor, the soul receives the mechanism for its thought processes, including the powers of logic, reasoning, organization and intellect. Finally, in Yesod/Foundation, the soul acquires the patterns of evolutionary inheritance, instinctual memory, subconsciousness and the collective unconscious that prepare it for human birth. These imprints include our basic instinctual needs, psychic connection to the animal soul of terrestrial life forms, sex drive and ability to create and reproduce patterns of all sorts, e.g., physical, mental and emotional patterns. Subconsciousness makes no judgments and tends to automatically reproduce whatever is repeatedly fed into it.

Our power to create is an awesome consequence of being created in God's image and likeness in that we can do what God does on our own limited level. Our creativity is a divine gift and power for which we're responsible in how we choose to use it. Patterns created by us and held in Yesod take on a life of their own and become the automatic, subconscious programming or operating system for our human personality and ego-identity in Malkuth. Our separate-self identity develops as we experience duality and the various pairs of opposites in human ground. Patterns involving undue attachment to our separate-self ego-identity and its self-centered desires are primary obstacles to our soul's accessing its divine inheritance, since these self-centered patterns tend to deny or preclude our connection to spiritual ground.

Each person's programming or operating system in Yesod consists of unconscious personality patterns formed of subtle astral matter that function automatically outside one's conscious awareness and control. Some of these unconscious patterns, like our basic instinctual needs and capacities for bodily awareness, emotion and thought, are human nature's preprogramming that we're born with. These unconscious patterns have been created for us by Nature through the long process of human evolution. Other patterns in the human personality's operating system are learned, chosen, created or acquired by us, e.g., derived from early-life imprints, basic instinctual needs, and social, religious and cultural conditioning.

The creation of each unique human personality is a complex process involving the formation of both conscious and unconscious patterns of thought, feeling and action that define the individual's character, style and goals in life. Though many key patterns are set early in life, each human personality is capable of changing and evolving throughout life. All unconscious personality patterns in an individual are not obstacles to human freedom and spiritual growth, only some of them are. Healthy personality patterns, be they conscious or unconscious, actually support our human and spiritual growth. As we outgrow our immature false self, the building up of our new self as a unique expression of the divine image creates new patterns in the soul. This is the work of Christ and the Holy Spirit in us, which needs our cooperation and brings us into conscious possession of our divine inheritance.

The imprints of our divine inheritance precede those of our human inheritance and, as we evolve spiritually, tend to become unconscious or automatic personality patterns. Our divine inheritance occupies a higher, deeper and more permanent place in the soul as the imprint of

God's image, will and plan for us. The patterns of our human inheritance and personality, though relatively fixed, are less permanent, subject to change and need to change as we grow to maturity and evolve from false self to true self. The patterns of our divine inheritance, received in the Spiritual/Moral Triad, are immutable and permanent because they're grounded in the eternal values, qualities and law of the divine in us. Each of us is intended to become a unique expression of the divine image, a kind of individual filter or instrument through which the qualities and consciousness of non-created Reality may express into created reality.

In contrast to our divine image, the unconscious personality patterns of our human inheritance in the Personality/Astral Triad are the mutable expressions of an evolving work-in-progress. For example, how we experience and express our basic instinctual needs changes dramatically as we evolve from infancy into maturity, and from false self to true self. This happens as we learn to pursue spiritual values and goals, outgrow the immaturities of childish happiness programs and gradually awaken into our true self or life in Christ.

Our spiritual goal of rebirth in Christ requires a conversion of the soul's Personality/Astral Triad into a true reflection and expression of the qualities and values of the Spiritual/Moral Triad above it. This amounts to the integration of our human nature into our divine nature, our false self into our true self, and our divided human personality into the unifying divine image in our soul. It means that the Spheres of the Personality/Astral Triad are to evolve into harmonious alignment with the corresponding higher Spheres in the Spiritual/Moral Triad. That is, our will, emotions, imagination and desire nature in Netzach are to become inspired and guided by the higher ideals, wisdom and values of Chesed. Our intellectual reasoning, judgment and thought processes in Hod are to be illumined by the clarity of understanding, conscience and discriminating intelligence in Geburah. And the instinctual energies, animal soul, unconscious personality patterns, subconscious mind and archetypes in Yesod are to come under the rulership of the soul's Central Archetype in Tiphareth: Christ, the King. The completion of this inner growth process implements what we pray for in the Lord's Prayer when we say, "Thy kingdom come,

Thy will be done, on earth as it is in heaven": "earth" being Malkuth/Kingdom and the Personality/Astral Triad, and "heaven" being the Spiritual/Moral and Supernal Triads.

If we reflect on this, the above line from the Lord's Prayer alludes allegorically to the cultivation and fruition of our rebirth in Christ on the Tree of Life. Through this spiritual rebirth, our soul is transformed into "a new creation" (2 Cor. 5:17). Given this description and goal, the practical question arises, how do we get from where we are now in human ground to there in spiritual ground and the treasure of our divine inheritance? How does the flawed, divided organization of our human personality or false self come to be redeemed, transformed and integrated into our true self, the divine image in our soul? How is God's will to be accomplished in us? The short answer, already given, is that our rebirth in Christ is the work of God in us that requires our willing consent, faithful trust and full cooperation.

To answer this question in more detail and depth, we need to take a closer look at the parameters of human existence (Four Fruits of the Fall), our basic instinctual needs and their distortions into emotional happiness programs or pathological unconscious personality patterns. We'll need to grasp the formation, programming and operating system of the human personality in Malkuth and the Personality/Astral Triad, its obstacles to spiritual growth and how these may be changed into our true self (life in Christ) and fulfillment of God's plan. As Thomas Keating's conceptual background for Centering Prayer tells us, our primary obstacles are the unconscious personality patterns that comprise the false-self system, i.e., our childish "emotional programs for happiness that can't possibly work" and over-identification with the mistaken separate-self identity that attends them.[1]

II

There are certain governing patterns of Nature functioning in Malkuth and the Personality/Astral Triad that are inherent to our human condition and nature. These have been described at length in *Human Ground, Spiritual Ground*[2] as the "Four Fruits of the Fall," our basic instinctual needs and the conflict between our false self and true self.

For purposes of this book, I'll briefly outline them here, adding some new material that's relevant to our discussion in the context of the Tree of Life:

Being subject to the Four Fruits of the Fall and our basic instinctual needs are inevitable realities of life in human ground. The four fruits are basic existential conditions or parameters to which we're all subject, and our basic instinctual needs are hardwired energy patterns of motivation and desire that run our unconscious operating system. The complex of ways in which we experience and relate to the fruits and our basic needs derives from our responses to them and creates the unconscious patterns that govern our personality. These patterns develop as we grow up and may be set or changed as we choose our priorities and direction in life. On the other hand, the core patterns of our basic instinctual needs and fruits of the Fall are realities and conditions we cannot change. What may change is how we relate to them. That is, we may change our attitudes and responses to them; and we may, with God's help, outgrow their unnecessary limitations as our personality and consciousness evolve from human ground to spiritual ground. This is a profound learning process in the soul.

The Four Fruits of the Fall are physical, motivational, moral/ethical and psychological parameters of our life and identity in human ground. These four fruits are: death/change; sex/desire; good/evil choices; and our aloneness/incompleteness apart from God. Our existence as human beings is limited by these parameters in time and space where nothing is permanent. All that we have and are is subject to the fruit of death/change in time and space. All energy in created reality is in motion, which means change, and this is a necessary condition in order for evolution and growth to occur. The death or ending of one life or condition within a life is always followed by the birth of another. This is a universal pattern throughout Nature and on the Tree of Life in both the visible and invisible worlds. How we relate to death/change is a measure of our awareness and maturity in the acceptance of actual reality.

The fruit of sex/desire expresses the fact that we all have to deal with and relate to our creativity and the instinctual life-force energy in us, and we all have desires that motivate us to action. Wherever we desire or come to desire is where we may be tempted. Where we desire is where we care and this caring of emotional involvement is what gives meaning to our life, or the lack of it. We are all seeking some form of gratification, happiness or fulfillment and we all have to deal with the creative energy and impulses of sexuality within us. Sexuality, as energy and image, is the imprint of creativity. It symbolizes union or oneness with its object and expresses in various ways on all levels of our being: physical, vital, emotional, mental, psychic, social and spiritual. Appreciating how this is so calls for some thoughtful reflection and reveals the subtle power of symbolism in affecting our thoughts, desires and actions.

The fruit of good/evil choices relates to sex/desire in terms of what we desire and the moral/ethical decisions we make in pursuing our desires. When we have to choose between getting what we want and doing what's right, this challenges us and how we respond to the challenge serves to invest our life with positive or negative meaning on the spiritual level. The nature of this meaning depends on what we value most and what we choose to do to get what we want. Having to make good/evil choices is a basis of our relative free will, and it's inevitable that we have to make moral/ethical decisions in how we live our lives, treat others and pursue our desires. We also have to make good/evil choices in terms of how we treat our self, God and God's creation. There's a complex of reciprocal relations among these things, e.g., how we treat others affects how we treat our self and vice versa.

What's the difference between good and evil? The principle of Good says "Yes" to life and God's plan for our spiritual growth and creation's perfection. The principle of Evil says "No" to life and seeks to undermine God's plan and spiritual evolution, usually under the guise of deceptions that promise to fulfill desires at the expense of moral/ethical integrity. The agenda and practice of Good involves the promotion of love, truth and freedom for all. The way of Evil deprives us of love, truth and freedom while using, promoting and delighting in hatred, lies and slavery. Good is essentially creative while evil is ultimately destructive.

As mentioned earlier regarding the divine plan versus the Qlippoth or lower abyss of destruction, both Good and Evil seek return to non-created Reality, but by opposite routes. Good seeks return by way of God's plan through the progressive awakening of the divine image and our life in Christ. Good affirms life and desires "to be." Evil negates life and chooses "not to be." So the hidden or ultimate agenda of Evil is to pursue return to non-created Reality by the downward way of corruption, degradation, perversion, disintegration, insanity, death and destruction, i.e., by way of the Qlippoth. All our good/evil choices in human ground move us in one of these two directions—toward health or illness, life or death, creation or destruction, "to be" or "not to be." As imperfect human beings, we're all relative combinations of good and evil tendencies and personality patterns—sometimes we move in one direction, other times we move in the other. True self-knowledge involves learning the truth of this in our soul.

The fourth fruit of the Fall is our experience of existential aloneness/incompleteness apart from God. This fruit is symbolized in Genesis 3 by Adam and Eve's expulsion from Paradise and the Lord God's presence after they ate the "forbidden fruit" that gave them (us) "knowledge of good and evil" (conscience and awareness of the pairs of opposites), knowledge of their nakedness (sex/desire), and subjection to death/change in physical time and space. The "forbidden fruit" gives rise to the soul's loss of primal unity and innocence, and to the awakening of our separate-self consciousness apart from God. This loss of conscious connection to God gives rise to a vacant "hole in the soul," a haunting sense of incompleteness and of something essential missing, giving rise to the longings of sex/desire and a relentless spiritual hunger to fill the hole in, so we may again feel whole and complete.

As human beings, we are unconsciously driven to seek communion and union with whatever we believe will give us completion and wholeness. This compelling motivation is reflected in the longing for all we desire. It's our longing for satisfaction. In the intuitive language of unconscious symbolism drawn from Nature, sexual union represents all unions, i.e., union with whatever we desire. On the deepest level, sexual imagery represents spiritual integration of the soul's feminine and masculine energies into inner completion and wholeness. Hence, this mysterious symbolism suggests not only intense pleasure but the ideal intimacy, love and fulfillment we eternally seek, but which may be gained permanently only in union with God, i.e., only in the soul's Spiritual/Moral Triad and beyond.

The hole in the soul of our existential aloneness/incompleteness cries out through the longing of each desire we pursue in efforts to find happiness and resolve our dilemma of inner emptiness, which is the predicament of the false-self and its inherent insufficiency. Since the false separate-self sense is inherently divided and incomplete, no amount of fulfilled egocentric desires can permanently satisfy or resolve its dilemma. The only real solution is to transform and transcend the false self via rebirth into our true self and life in Christ. The answer will never be found in Malkuth and the Personality/Astral Triad apart from God. This is a great practical truth, heart-knowledge or ignorance of which may make the crucial difference between wisdom and folly in how we order our priorities, desires and choices.

III

The Four Fruits of the Fall (death/change, sex/desire, good/evil choices and aloneness/incompleteness apart from God) frame the context in which we experience our basic instinctual needs, which are primary, inborn expressions of the fruit of sex/desire in our soul. Our basic instinctual needs may be identified as security/survival/safety; sensation/pleasure; affection/esteem/approval; power/control; and intimacy/belonging. These needs are inherent to human nature and our soul's longing for spiritual growth. They are unconscious patterns of motivation and desire that underlie the formation and expression of our personality. Three of them, security/survival/safety, affection/esteem/approval and power/control, evolve from the three primary energy centers or Spheres in the Personality/Astral Triad as follows:

Security/survival/safety evolves out of Yesod, the instinctive energy center of automatic patterns, memory and the animal soul. Affection/esteem/approval evolves out of Netzach, the emotional energy center of imagination, desire and will. And power/control evolves out of Hod, the mental Sphere of intellectual concepts, thoughts, ideas, logic, reasoning, organization and analysis. Our other two basic instinctual needs, sensation/pleasure and intimacy/ belong-ing, may be experienced in conjunction with each other and in relation to the other three. Intimacy/belonging includes the social and spiritual dimensions of our life. Our basic needs are core aspects of our human inheritance and, as we evolve spiritually, they become vehicles for the manifestation of our spiritual inheritance as well, especially our need for intimacy/belonging in relation to others, self and God.

Our basic instinctual needs are interrelated and have to be met to some minimal degree if we're to survive, grow and enjoy health and wellbeing in life. These needs are especially acute in early life when we're most helpless, vulnerable and dependent on others (e.g., our par-ents) to meet our needs. Our early sense of self develops around these needs and our drive to get them met. This early sense of self is totally self-centered and develops into a separate-self sense of ego-identity as we grow up. Its sense of identity and perceptions of self and reality are supported by cultural conditioning and by the unconscious personal-ity patterns that underlie and form within it for better or worse as it develops over time.

Our evolving sense of self is dominated and driven by the instinc-tual needs and by various powerful positive and negative emotions that are activated when our needs are either gratified or frustrated. These powerful emotions are also activated when we *imagine* our needs are being gratified or frustrated, which demonstrates the creative power of the soul's imaging faculty in Netzach. When needs are gratified, we experience pleasure and are programmed to want more when the need naturally arises. When needs are frustrated or abused, we experi-ence pain and, to compensate, are programmed to want or demand an inordinate, exaggerated amount of gratification beyond what our legitimate needs naturally require. We may also program our self with irrational anger or fear, wanting revenge or protection from the frustration, trauma and pain we've suffered. In this way, pathological unconscious personality patterns develop in Yesod, trapping our life-force energy while blocking our human and spiritual growth.

It works like this: when real or imagined frustrations or abuses of basic instinctual needs are experienced in early life, the unbear-able pain of these experiences is repressed into the unconscious and warehoused in the physical body (Malkuth). Since there is no passage of time in the unconscious, the pain of our repressed experiences of deprivation/abuse, and our primitive emotional reactions to them, remain exactly the same as when originally repressed, affecting us unconsciously as we grow up and move through life. This repression ties up a lot of our life-force energy, retarding personal and emotional development while creating a continuing state of unconscious psychological bondage in the soul. Such repression is continual food for the false self.

Once repression takes place, drives or programs to compensate for the felt traumas of deprivation/abuse are set up in the unconscious energy centers of our basic instinctual needs in the Personality/Astral Triad, primarily in Yesod/Foundation in each of the relevant Sephiroth (each Sephira containing a smaller Tree of Life within itself). The personality's unconscious drives or programs for compensation are living structures of subtle astral matter made up of imagery and powered by affect. These living structures motivate a person to pursue the enactment and completion of their corresponding patterns in the imagery and relationships of one's outer life. Unconscious symbolism plays a key role in this process.

The personality's unconscious drives or patterns for compensation distort and exaggerate our basic instinctual needs beyond their natural healthy ways of functioning. These compulsions to compensate are charged and powered by the strong emotions of pain and pleasure stored in the instinctual energy centers. Hence, they develop into unconscious personality patterns or programs for happiness that will dominate us for the rest of our lives, unless some deep inner healing takes place. Together with the personality's exaggerated separate-self sense, the living structures of its unconscious happiness programs form the basic core and operating system of the false self. Due to its self-centered nature, which bolsters the false self, each person's unconscious complex of compensatory drives and emotional happiness programs sets the stage for serious hidden obstacles to one's human and spiritual growth.

Once established, self-centered emotional happiness programs in the unconscious become top priorities for us, though we may not consciously know what they are or be aware of this. Such personal agendas tend to oppose our higher human and spiritual values by reinforcing egoistic selfishness and functioning as idolatrous substitutes for God. In other words, God takes a lower priority to them in the order of importance of what we actually want in life. We may or may not be conscious of this. These unconscious programs for happiness and the automatic emotional reactions that accompany them function as unhealthy addictions and compulsions, dominating our thoughts, feelings and actions. We are unconsciously driven to pursue their gratification, even at the cost of violating conscience and the legitimate rights and needs of others; hence, their opposition to higher human and spiritual values.

Our negative unconscious personality patterns (happiness programs) are living structures in the Personality/Astral Triad coded in the symbolic language of images charged with the energy of will, desire and various powerful emotions that underlie and motivate much of our conscious behavior. There's an unconscious drive to match the energized symbols in the unconscious with corresponding imagery in one's outer life and relationships. When this is accomplished in a positive way as desired—that is, when we get what we want—one experiences temporary pleasure, joy and happiness. When it's experienced in a negative way, i.e., when happiness programs are frustrated, one overreacts and falls under the sway of various afflictive emotions, e.g., grief, anger, pride, envy, lust, fear, jealousy, guilt, depression, and so on. As afflictive emotions are triggered, we tend to think and act out of them quite unconsciously.

When one overreacts or over-compensates out of afflictive emotions, these are sure indications of false-self pathology in action where one's psychological buttons are pushed and emotional strings are pulled by the power of unconscious imagery energized with affect.

Hence, to consciously realize what's going on, it's important to take a step back and view one's experiences and situation objectively and from more than one perspective. Next, we may do well to reflect on the reciprocal relationships between consciousness and the unconscious together with how the power and functioning of symbolism in our outer life and relationships are affecting our inner psychology and spiritual life. Such honest inner reflection carried on over time can be a means to new self-knowledge, understanding and freedom. This process may also be facilitated by having a reliable friend or guide to share it with.

As mentioned above, self-centered emotional happiness programs rooted in Yesod, i.e., in the unconscious, are unhealthy distortions and exaggerations of our legitimate instinctual needs. These happiness programs become primary obstacles to our spiritual growth, once we consciously decide to pursue the spiritual journey. They are like false gods or goals of the ego that we place preciousness into in opposition to the higher human and divine values of our spiritual nature. Our childish programs for happiness are false because they inevitably fail us as well as enslave us. It makes no difference in the long run whether we get what we want or not because their gratifications are temporary; they block our growth and we remain bound to their limitations and afflictive emotions.

Emotional happiness programs fail us because they're based on false perceptions of reality and because they do not address the true needs of our soul. Such conscious or unconscious personality patterns are actually programs for human misery. They're inadequate substitutes for our true needs and relationship to the divine. The unique complex of emotional happiness programs in each person, rooted in the Personality/Astral Triad, forms the living structure of her or his false-self system. The false self tends to over-compensate and over-react in relation to whatever stimulates its programs for happiness. Each person's false self is the result of where we've gotten stuck in our human growth process from early life onward. It's something we need to outgrow that's ultimately an illusion. It's who we may think we are but not who we really are; as Thomas Keating says, it's a "homemade self" and not the true self of our spiritual nature and life in God.

IV

We'll now look at the basic instinctual needs whose distortions and exaggerations into unconscious personality patterns form the inner motivation of the false-self system. The first and most primary of these is our need for security/survival/safety, which grows out of the universal survival instinct in all living organisms. What could be more fundamental to life in Malkuth than our need to survive here, to learn and grow, to flourish and prosper? These are the essential requirements, the prerequisites for remaining and realizing meaningful purpose in human ground. All of our basic instinctual needs, in their healthy, life-affirming expressions, are in the service of this goal—which extends through life in human ground and society up into the higher values, meaning and purpose of spiritual ground following God's plan for creation.

If our security/survival/safety need is deprived, abused or experienced as unmet in early life, an emotional agenda of symbolic patterns to compensate may be set up in the unconscious (Yesod/Foundation). Consequently, in adult life we'll be compulsively driven to seek an inordinate amount of things symbolizing security/survival/safety in our culture—e.g., more and more material wealth, possessions, toys, insurance policies and medical reassurances of our health and longevity. We unconsciously, and to some degree consciously, identify these things with happiness, wellbeing and feeling secure. Unfortunately, acquiring more and more symbols of security/survival/safety does not change the childish program for happiness in our unconscious.

When unmet needs are acutely felt, the child in us has little, if any, sense of moderation and our demands for gratification, if unchecked, become extreme and fantastic. No matter how much wealth or whatever we may amass, it's never enough because our childish happiness programs are insatiable. It's like an appetite without limit craving more and more so the hungry soul's empty hole may be filled in, which it never can be by these means

When we don't get what we want to gratify our security/survival/safety happiness program, we suffer various afflictive emotions, such as the insecurity, helplessness, fear, panic or rage that engendered the compulsion to begin with. When we do get what we want, e.g., more money, a new possession, etc., our feeling of gratification is relatively short lived because our childish happiness program will refuse to rest satisfied and continues to demand more. Why is this?

It's because the false happiness program does not and cannot address our true need beyond what we legitimately require in the way of security/survival/safety. The true need of our hole in the soul is our need for love which is ultimately our need for God. Material things cannot address this need. So, as the novelty of each new acquisition wears off, we again find our self feeling empty, incomplete and wanting something else that's newer or better. Sadly, we remain ignorant of the fact that faith in our security/survival/safety happiness program is misplaced and based on false unconscious assumptions.

When our need for sensation/pleasure is distorted into an emotional happiness program, this unconscious personality pattern may lead us to unhealthy extremes in various areas of human enjoyment, often in conjunction with happiness programs related to other basic needs, e.g., affection/esteem, power/control or intimacy/belonging. The healthy expression of our need for sensation/pleasure is meant to affirm life's beauty and goodness, to provide us with fun, laughter, drama and the enjoyable stimulation of our mind, emotions, body and spirit. All our basic instinctual needs are sources of healthy sensation/pleasure when met and gratified as intended by Nature. In this sense, our need for sensation/pleasure is a byproduct of our other basic needs as well as a legitimate need in its own right. Sensation/pleasure reveals the wonder and goodness of human life, which is a precious gift meant to be enjoyed.

When sensation/pleasure becomes a false-self happiness program, we tend to become greedy and overindulge in food, sex, entertainment, excitement, alcohol, drugs or other things in ways that are destructive to our health, personal freedom, important relationships and peace of mind. Self-indulgent hedonism is not the answer to life's ultimate questions and various forms of sensation/pleasure may be misused to escape boredom or as distraction from personal issues we really need to deal with. Rather than increasing our quality of life, too much sensation/pleasure actually diminishes it, exhausting our nerves, dulling our sensitivity and curtailing our natural ability to enjoy life in the present moment. Depending too much on external sources of sensation/pleasure is an inadequate substitute for meaningful relationships with others, our self or God. It weakens us, may reduce us to slavery in the dependencies of addiction, and causes us to lose touch with the inner wealth and worth we already possess.

When our basic need for affection/esteem/approval is distorted and exaggerated into an emotional happiness program, we crave acceptance, wanting everyone to like or respect us and reassure us of our value. We may try to impress others in various ways to earn their admiration or affection. We may also try this with God. Or we may enter and remain in abusive, exploitative or codependent relationships, trying to get our exaggerated emotional needs met. One example is the "people pleaser" who tries to gain acceptance and affection by serving the desires and needs of others while ignoring one's own. All these strategies and others are fated to fail because no matter how much attention, admiration, affection, esteem or approval we get, it's never enough since healthy self-esteem is an inside job requiring the kind of self-knowledge and self-respect that come from being true to our self and conscience.

Our basic need for power/control is essentially our need for personal freedom and independence. This need may be fully met only by embracing our utter dependence on God, our true self and the wisdom of conscience. When power/control becomes an emotional happiness program, as it often does, we're driven to seek power/control not only in our own life but also over situations and other people by such means as persuasion, manipulation, seduction, lying, subtle intimidation or outright bullying. Seeking various positions of authority and power in society is a common strategy employed by individuals driven by power/control happiness programs. Again, no matter how much power/control we manage to gain in order to feel secure, successful, happy, free, or to impress others, it's never enough. There are always more people or situations to control and more competitors to contend with. In such situations, we may find no peace, love or lasting satisfaction. We're unable to let our self go in personal relationships by trusting another or being vulnerable. Consequently, life may become a meaningless, stressful wasteland of hollow victories, separate-self alienation and loneliness.

Intimacy/belonging is an outer social need and an inner spiritual need. Outwardly, intimacy/belonging is our need for a sense of place in this world, where we care, are cared for and belong. We may meet this need through primary human relationships and by identification and loyalty to our home culture or society, i.e., the various groups to which we belong. Inwardly, intimacy/belonging is our need for love and closeness to our self, certain special others in our life, and in relation to God. As love is the soul-force of intimacy, to know and be known in communion and union is the essence of intimacy/belonging on the spiritual level. We may pursue this through deep self-knowledge, mutual knowledge and self-disclosure with those we love, and most profoundly and completely in our relationship with God, who knows us through and through.

All forms of authentic intimacy expose us and make us vulnerable. Consequently, all personal forms of intimacy/belonging require a high level of trust or faith in the other as well as honesty in self-disclosure. This entails taking risks by opening our self to uncertainty, potential disappointment, possible betrayal and wounding. In other words, it requires a certain measure of courage and willingness to be vulnerable by being exposed and seen as we truly are; that is, to see our self as we truly are, to allow another person to really see us, and to be humble and intimate in God's presence and the deeper self-knowledge this brings. Love, as it blossoms in the soul, makes us humble and grateful, free and alive, blissful and glorious—all at the same time. Authentic love blesses us with the precious, liberating inner wealth of feeling whole and complete in our self. Such is the higher fulfillment of our spiritual need for intimacy/belonging.

When we're afraid to trust and be vulnerable, due to betrayal or hurt in the past, then it's not easy to enter a deeply intimate relationship with another person. In lieu of such intimacy, we may prefer the safety of more shallow, less fully engaged relationships. In our relationship with our self, there's apparently less risk of betrayal, though one should not underestimate the machinations of the false self and the dark side of our personality. Our inner relationship with God is the one place where there's no risk or danger of betrayal, loss or abandonment, since God knows us completely, loves us unconditionally and is not subject to the limitations of a false self or perverse dark side. However, increasing intimacy with God does challenge us to increasing trust and faith in the divine action as it reveals us to our self and does what's needed to purify, heal and renew us.

Our true home, where we ultimately belong, is in the light of God's presence shining in the soul. This light holds a boundless treasure and depth of eternal life and love. Intimacy with God, as develops in contemplative prayer, is the natural way through inner darkness into the dawning light of God's presence—which has unlimited degrees and qualities of radiance that may, by God's grace, manifest in our consciousness to heal and transform us.

When our need for intimacy/belonging is distorted into emotional happiness programs, we tend to pursue various forms of pseudo-intimacy, ranging from the shallow to the perverse. This may involve any kind of relationship we have or care about, e.g., with other people, our self, groups and even with God. False-self intimacy is essentially a substitute for authentic intimacy—which opens the heart, revealing us to our self and one another. Fear of the vulnerability and self-disclosure authentic intimacy requires may motivate one to hide and retreat into the seeming safety of pseudo-intimacy.

When psychological projections and ego-fantasy distort our perceptions of personal relationships and activities, or when we over-identify with cultural conditioning and various groups, the situation is ripe for false-self intimacy to develop. Such pseudo-intimacy can be quite deceptive. It generally clings to the surface, depends on fantasy, and is unable to really see or contact the depth dimension in oneself or another. Pseudo-intimacy also tends to identify with the herd instinct of conformity to the consensus values and views of a group, seeking comfort and meaning by following the crowd and one's own imaginings. Such false, superficial intimacy is a lonely place to be, as it's a shallow compromise that can never meet the soul's deep need for love and belonging.

Happiness programs that distort our need for intimacy/belonging may also converge with happiness programs related to other of our basic instinctual needs. For example, we may identify and feel intimate with our physical comforts and possessions (security/survival/safety); the pleasures we enjoy (sensation/pleasure); our agendas for affection/esteem/approval (which ties into intimacy/belonging) and power/control. All of these things and others may serve as self-centered substitutes for authentic intimacy/belonging in relation to self, others, God and God's creation.[3]

V

Our important group identifications, social learning and cultural conditioning address our need for intimacy/belonging and bring us into the collective, social dimension of the false self's personality patterns. This is true to whatever degree these internalized outer influences express human nature's flaws and false-self values, alongside their positive life-affirming qualities. Cultural conditioning is an essential part of our human identity and inheritance. It involves being programmed with a learned identity and the values, world view and beliefs of the society in which we live.

Over-identification with the cultural conditioning of family, peers, ethnic group, race, religion, learned sexual identity, and other roles may be used to help compensate for a lack of intimacy/belonging and fulfillment in our personal or spiritual lives. Being part of a group gives us a sense of belonging and through the group-mind we may experience a semblance of meaningful intimacy with others. Cultural conditioning teaches us certain attitudes, beliefs, values and ways of interpreting life. It gives us the orientation of a particular perspective on the world. By sharing attitudes, beliefs, values, tastes and views in common with other members of society, we're able to understand each other to some degree and feel we belong to a common group. Hence, cultural conditioning relates directly to our social need for intimacy/belonging.

It allows us to fit into society but also carries the limitations of our group's collective false-self system and values, e.g., biases and prejudices. As the soul evolves from identification with the false self into awareness of the true self, an identity shift from human ground to spiritual ground takes place. This identity shift develops our unique individuality and changes how we relate to the group-mind and cultural conditioning, which become more like clothes we put on than our actual body that wears them.

Instead of regarding cultural conditioning as an essential basis of our identity, we come to experience it more as an outer role or set of roles we play in relating to society and the world. In shifting our sense of identity to the spiritual center of our being, we come to understand the various values, world views, beliefs and roles derived from cultural conditioning to be humanly created things that we temporarily adopt and use to function in society, as opposed to regarding them as the essential basis of our core identity. This enables us to view the values and beliefs of groups other than our own more objectively.

We may imagine the inner transformation from false self to true self as a movement of the Spiritual/Moral Triad down into the Personality/Astral Triad. This imagery suggests a symbolic recapitulation in our soul of Christ's descent into human ground in the person of Jesus. The blossoming of our life in Christ is what Thomas Keating has called "inner resurrection." This takes place over time as we awaken into the consciousness and identity of our true self. Until this identity shift from human personality and false self into true self occurs, we're bound to be influenced and possibly dominated by unconscious personality patterns of cultural conditioning, afflictive emotions and emotional programs for happiness.

VI

The combination of the Four Fruits of the Fall (death/change, sex/desire, good/evil choices and aloneness/incompleteness apart from God) together with our basic instinctual needs (security/survival/safety, sensation/pleasure, affection/esteem/approval, power/control and intimacy/belonging) sets the stage for innumerable dramatic possibilities in human life and relationships. Each human personality is unique and may never be repeated, just as historical times and events in society and culture are unique and may not be repeated. This fact expresses the awesome diversity of God's creativity on the Tree of Life where infinite possibilities exist. Among these possibilities is the inherent potential of each individual soul to evolve into a unique conscious expression of the divine image.

Everything changes in time and space through the continuing flow of energy in created reality following the laws that govern it: these laws being an expression of the divine will. Though the same patterns may be repeated on and on in time and space, they're always repeated differently under differing conditions out of which all possibilities may eventually manifest. Hence, each moment, as well as each individual soul, human personality and relationship is unique to its place in time and may never be duplicated in exactly the same way.

This uniqueness is certainly true regarding the expressions of our conscious and unconscious personality patterns. As stated earlier, there is, in each person, a set of unconscious personality patterns that underlie much of one's conscious and unconscious behavior and experience. Some of these patterns are inborn components of human nature and the human condition that do not change, though how we understand and relate to them changes as we learn and grow. Other personality patterns are created by us in response to life experiences and our inherent patterns. The patterns we create inevitably change as we grow up and evolve from human ground into spiritual ground.

The fruits of the Fall and our basic instinctual needs are obvious examples of human nature's inborn patterns. Our conscious and unconscious habits of thought, feeling and action, the desires and dreams we pursue together with our emotional responses to their gratifications or frustrations, our belief system and evolving sense of identity are examples of personality patterns that do change. The crucial dynamic of individual free will plays a pivotal role in creating, maintaining and transforming our changeable personality patterns as well as how we relate to those patterns we can't change.

As we enter separate-self consciousness in human ground, the dynamic of free will facing good/evil choices launches us on life's adventure. We've been given freedom to choose and create our destiny within the limits of our existential circumstances, along with responsibility for our choices and their consequences. Whether we choose freely and consciously, or blindly and unconsciously, human life forces us to make moral/ethical decisions and we're destined to experience and become the consequences of those choices. This is our lot in human ground (Malkuth and the Personality/Astral Triad), which is the place of human creativity on the Tree of Life.

In this chapter, we've described human nature's unconscious personality patterns in terms of the four parameters of human existence (fruits of the Fall), our basic instinctual needs and their unhealthy distortions into emotional happiness programs that trap us in separate-self consciousness, preventing us from realizing our true self and spiritual inheritance. In the following chapter, we'll look at the hidden mechanisms of our personality patterns as living structures of energy, imagery, habit and desire in the Personality/Astral Triad and physical body. In doing this, we'll need to nuance the inner workings of the Tree of Life in terms of the smaller Trees within the individual Sephiroth and how they relate to the Tree as a whole. We are here describing an invisible inner process that may be represented and interpreted in a variety of ways, e.g., as in Western and Eastern ideas of philosophy, psychology, metaphysics and religion, all of which we may learn and benefit from. The Tree of Life model as presented here is simply one approach to this.

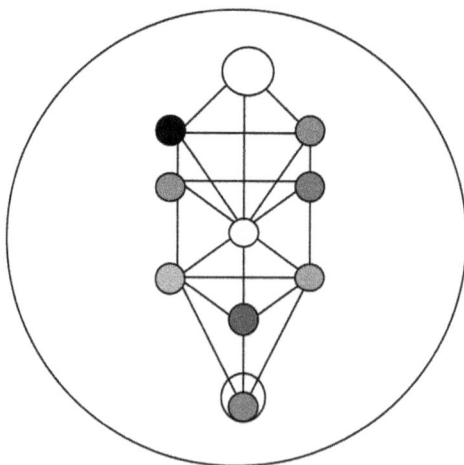

Smaller Tree Within a Sephira

9

PERSONALITY PATTERNS ON THE TREE OF LIFE

I

It's not possible to be born human without suffering wounding in our basic instinctual needs, real or imagined. As we move through infancy and toddlerhood into childhood and adolescence and on into physical adulthood, further wounding, e.g., from injury, illness, deprivation, neglect, abuse, rejection, disappointment, loss or abandonment, is liable to occur. The overwhelming anxiety, pain, fear, guilt or anger tied to these unpleasant negative experiences causes them to be repressed into the unconscious, where programs for compensation are created in the subtle energy centers (Sephiroth) of our basic instinctual needs. These programs for compensation and the afflictive emotions tied to them become the self-centered happiness programs that motivate our false-self system. They are further complicated by the effects of social learning, cultural conditioning and over-identification with various groups in which we participate.

Programs to compensate for unmet basic needs are set up in the energy centers or Sephiroth of the Personality/Astral Triad that correspond to those needs. That is, frustrations of the need for security/survival/safety are recorded in Yesod on the Middle Pillar of the Tree at the bottom of the Personality/Astral Triad; deprivations of our mental need for power/control register in Hod at the bottom of the Pillar of Severity; and abuses of our emotional need for affection/esteem/approval lodge in Netzach at the bottom of the Pillar of Mercy. These happiness programs tend to have negative impacts on the healthy growth and functioning of our human personality and the Sephiroth that contain them.

Our unmet needs for vital sensation/pleasure (Yesod) and social-spiritual intimacy/belonging (associated with Tiphareth, the heart center) may circulate among the Sephiroth of the Personality/Astral Triad, lodging in the specific Sephiroth associated with the types of experiences involved; that is, whether they are primarily physical, vital, emotional, mental, psychic, social or spiritual. The memories of both pleasant and unpleasant experiences, and drives to compensate for real or imagined wounds of deprivation, neglect and abuse, are held in the Yesod/Foundation of the smaller Tree of Life within specific Sephira of the Personality/Astral Triad. All of these unresolved experiences and memories are concomitantly warehoused in various parts of the physical body, brain and nervous system, i.e., in Malkuth, and may affect one's physical health as well as one's psycho-spiritual wellbeing.

Happiness programs often involve more than one Sephira. For example, the need to compensate for strong feelings of insecurity in Yesod may also carry over into desires for power/control in Hod and cravings for affection/esteem/approval in Netzach. All Sephiroth in the Personality/Astral Triad and on the Tree as a whole are in continual interaction and relationship with one another, exchanging energies and influencing one another as an organic whole. From this, we may see that the false self's happiness programs are also interrelated as a whole, working either in harmony or conflict with one another.

The actual structures and workings of the energies and Spheres on the Tree of Life are not limited to the three dimensions of physical time and space, as we may imagine them to be. The fact that there's a smaller Tree of Life contained within each of the ten Sephiroth hints at this because the smaller individual Sephiroth within each of the ten are actually not separate from the Sephiroth to which they correspond on the larger Tree. For example, the Tiphareth within the smaller Trees of the Personality/Astral-Triad Sephiroth are really not separate from the big Tiphareth in the Spiritual/Moral Triad of the larger Tree. Likewise, the Yesods in Hod, Netzach and the rest of the Tree are not separate from the larger Yesod in the Personality/Astral Triad. Hence, the actual functioning Tree does not conform to the normal dimensions of time and space in which we may visualize it. We are here using visual images to represent, in terms of the Tree of Life, what is essentially a mysterious invisible process in the soul.

So, on the Tree of Life, the unconscious personality patterns of the false self are housed in Yesod (the Sephira of patterns) in the three Sephiroth of the Personality/Astral Triad. Actual Yesod on the Middle Pillar and the two side Yesods in the smaller Trees within Hod (the Sphere of intellect) and Netzach (the Sphere of emotions) together contain the living patterns of the false self's core emotional happiness programs. These living unconscious personality patterns are composed of creative life-force energy formed by imagination and will into symbolic images of astral-matter expressing our desires for compensation. A radical transformation of these living images and structures of astral matter in the unconscious (Yesod) is required for the elimination of the false self to take place.

While they're strong and active in us, we are unconsciously compelled to attempt to match the inner symbolism of our happiness programs with corresponding symbolism involving various people, places, things and relationships in our outer life. This, in general, is how we try to meet the demands and fulfill the desires of our false self's emotional programs for happiness. It's essentially a symbolic game of trying to find and attain various things in our outer life that correspond to the inner symbolic happiness programs in the unconscious, i.e., the previously mentioned distortions and exaggerations of our basic instinctual needs. These happiness programs are living structures of subtle astral matter in the soul that need to be disempowered, dismantled and replaced if we're to gain freedom from their negative influences in our lives and relationships.

II

In addition to the flawed personality patterns that constitute the false-self system, healthy personality patterns related to our human and spiritual growth are also held in Yesod and the Spheres of the Personality/Astral Triad. These healthy patterns originate in Tiphareth in the Spiritual/Moral Triad. They come into expression as our intellect evolves in harmony with conscience, our emotional desire nature matures into alignment with higher human and spiritual values, and the passions of our instinctual animal nature are tamed and domesticated into the service of our true self and God's plan. As we grow up emotionally into free and responsible human adults, the raw material of our human nature gradually becomes an expression of our higher potentials for human and spiritual growth. This involves the practical development of physical, emotional, mental and social skills; and it involves a shift in our basic orientation in life from the self-centered egotism of childhood and adolescence into the higher perspectives of compassion and respect for the legitimate needs, rights and dignity of others.

The growing-up process of evolution into human and spiritual wellbeing involves an openness and receptivity in the Spheres of the Personality/Astral Triad to the higher humanizing influences of the corresponding Spheres in the Spiritual/Moral Triad. Human health, wellbeing and maturity require a harmonious alignment between the surface personality or ego-identity in the Personality/Astral Triad and the true self or divine image in our soul, which descends from the higher Spheres of the Spiritual/Moral Triad. A minimal meeting and satisfaction of our basic instinctual needs on the emotional level seems to be a prerequisite for this inner growth process to move forward. Hence, before our higher inner development may actually take place, our basic instinctual needs must be met to some degree and whatever in us that opposes this growth must be overcome, removed and replaced with healthy new patterns. To complete itself, this inner transformation has to take place in the Spheres of the Personality/Astral Triad; that is, our true self needs to be born in the personality's unconscious patterns and programming (Yesod), in our conscious intellectual outlook (Hod), and in our emotional desire nature (Netzach).

III

The healthy and unhealthy personality patterns held in Yesod, the Personality/Astral Triad, and also physiologically in Malkuth, are commonly known as habits of thought, feeling and action. The deepest of these habit patterns, held in the hidden recesses of Yesod, constitute the living foundation of one's personality and character. This inner foundation is a primary expression of our desire nature (Netzach) over time in terms of what we want and need on all levels, i.e., physical, emotional, mental, etc. An essential part of each personality's inner structure is how it copes and strives to compensate for the unhealed wounds and unmet needs of early life, childhood, adolescence and adulthood. Our inner wounds and programs to compensate tend to be layered on top of one another in chronological order.[1] As we've seen, the dysfunctional personality patterns held in Yesod form the basis of the false-self system that retards human and spiritual growth.

These inner obstacles are essentially habits of thought, feeling and action that express and reinforce the false self. The chief difficulty in dealing with such habit patterns and desires lies in the fact that their root-causes are hidden in the unconscious recesses of Yesod, where we do not have free, conscious access to them. When such habits of our making automatically control us against our conscious will, we may rightly call them pathological compulsions or addictions. What we do have conscious access to, if we'll pay attention, are our habitual and often automatic choices, together with the positive or negative results they produce in daily life and consciousness. To become better aware of our existential situation, we need to practice self-observation, take an inventory of our habit patterns, and then evaluate the results they create. Thus may we discover which habits we'd like to continue and which ones we need to eliminate to improve our quality of life.

Humans have rightly been called "creatures of habit." There's a variety of habit patterns associated with every level of the soul's functioning: physical, vital, emotional, mental, psychic, social and spiritual. All habits are developed and strengthened by repetition. Well-developed habits become automatic and tend to function on their own, subconsciously, without our thinking about them. Depending on what these automatic habits are, they may or may not be in our true interest. As the inner locus for each person's automatic habit patterns is in Yesod (the Sephira of patterns and "automatic consciousness"), they reside astrally in the Yesods of the small Trees of the Sephiroth in the Personality/Astral Triad.

One way of viewing habit patterns, especially those that enslave and cause us suffering, is in terms of addictions. Addictions are commonly regarded as pathological behavior patterns that compel us to act in ways that oppose our true needs and desires. The false self's happiness programs are an obvious example of such addictions on the psychological level. In his informative book, *Addiction and Grace*, Gerald May defines addiction as "a state of compulsion, obsession, or preoccupation that enslaves a person's will and desire." [2] Dr. May goes on to describe addiction as the attachment of our desire-energy to some specific behaviors, persons or objects in place of our deeper, truer needs and desires for authentic human and spiritual values (like love, truth, freedom and intimacy with another person or God).

In addition to tying up the energy of our will on the psychological level, addiction has a physiological component on the physical, neurological level in our brain and nervous system, where chemical and neurological activities compel us to repeat addictive behavior patterns. The neurological/biochemical aspect of addiction is how it manifests on the physical level of Malkuth, driving habit patterns of thought, feeling and action in tandem with their corresponding living images and energetic structures of subtle astral matter in Yesod. Thus, addictive behaviors involve both physical and psychological processes and may originate on either the neurological/biochemical or metaphysical levels of the soul. These two levels complement each other so that if one acts, its counterpart tends to react upon it.

A broader view of addiction is to see it as any behavior we do repeatedly that we can't stop doing. Under this definition, we are all addicts of one kind or another since there are certain things we need to keep doing in order to live. In this view, an addiction is any habit pattern that we're compelled to continue repeating for better or worse and whether we're aware of it or not. With this definition, we may distinguish between healthy and unhealthy addictions, rather than viewing all addictions as unhealthy. For example, we're all born addicted to our basic instinctual needs and we become subsequently addicted to various behavior patterns with which we try to satisfy those needs, e.g., breathing, eating, sleeping, exercise, work, play and our emotional programs for happiness.

Seen in this light, addictions are an inevitable part of being human and may be positive or negative, healthy or unhealthy, depending on their consequences. Our struggle with unhealthy addictions, once we become aware of them, is a struggle for personal and spiritual freedom. This is a struggle we need to undertake, if we're to be true to our self and God's plan for us. How may we change or overcome our unhealthy addictions, once we're aware of them? As Gerald May points out in *Addiction and Grace*, we need divine help to accomplish this. We need to see our unhealthy addictions for what they actually are, so we'll want to get rid of them. We need to starve them of energy by resisting them, withdrawing from them, renouncing and letting them go. Our will needs to act in concert with the divine action of grace in our soul to accomplish this. To overcome unhealthy addictions is not easy. It is to live through a kind of death and rebirth struggle, a dark night of the soul in Malkuth and the three Sephiroth of the Personality/Astral Triad.

IV

An ancient, traditional way of viewing unhealthy habit patterns that afflict and addict is in terms of motivation by unclean spirits, demons and devils. Contemporary cultural conditioning and modern scientific thought tend to associate belief in such unsavory creatures with ignorance and superstition, and often for good reason; but this in itself does not prove that such invisible nonphysical entities do not or cannot exist in some way. Ancient spiritual and modern scientific views are not always mutually exclusive and may express different, complementary ways of describing and interpreting some of the same phenomena, e.g., how these phenomena express on physical and nonphysical levels. Moral/ethical values are never out of date, and belief in both good and evil nonphysical entities influencing human health and behavior dates back to prehistory and may be found in all the world's religious and spiritual traditions, including Qabalah.

In the gospels, we read of Jesus casting out demons and unclean spirits that possess and afflict people as part of his healing ministry; these evil entities are portrayed as possessing consciousness and awareness of who Jesus is (see, for example, Mark 1:23–27, 32–34). The Christian Nicene Creed affirms belief in God as maker of "heaven and earth, of all things visible and invisible"; that is, belief in the reality of what our human senses perceive and what they cannot perceive. In Qabalah, the Spheres of the Personality/Astral, Spiritual/Moral and Supernal Triads are the invisible realms and dwelling places in God's creation where all that is unseen on earth exists, manifesting as darkness and light within the Absolute Consciousness of God's Limitless Light.

According to Qabalistic teaching, each Sephira on the Universal Tree of Life is a vast domain of created reality in which various types of conscious entities live and act. These invisible realms on the Tree may be compared to parallel universes at higher energy levels that coexist with Malkuth, our familiar physical Universe. There are, no doubt, innumerable categories of positive and negative conscious beings on the Tree, representing all stages of consciousness evolution and devolution, ranging from the darkest realms of the Abyss, Yesod and the Personality/Astral Triad (earth) up into the higher realms of increasing light in the Spiritual/Moral and Supernal Triads (heaven). This is a summary glimpse at the big picture of the Universal Tree, which contains all possibilities of reality and experience, creation and destruction, being and becoming within created reality.

What primarily concerns us in this chapter are those forces and influences in the Personality/Astral Triad that relate to our personality patterns of thought (Hod), feeling (Netzach), and action (Yesod and Malkuth). Many of these patterns originate in the Personality/Astral Triad itself and others may descend into the Personality/Astral Triad from the Spiritual/Moral Triad above it. These latter energies and influences are the inner impulses and inspirations of the Spirit that purify, heal and transform us, fueling human evolution's ascent into spiritual ground and the awakening of our divine inheritance.

V

The Personality/Astral Triad, together with Malkuth, constitutes the earthly realm of human creativity wherein humans possess the power to create and are intended to be co-creators with God, to fulfill the divine plan. The habits we create are an essential part of our personality patterns and we are responsible for both the positive and the negative results they produce. Our human ground is also the realm where the forces of good and evil, creation and destruction contend with each other to affirm or negate the goodness of life and our spiritual inheritance. Many of the nonphysical entities active in the Personality/Astral Triad are products of human creativity; that is, they're creations of human thought, will, desire, instinct and habit—manifesting in the Sephiroth of the Personality/Astral Triad.

Among the nonphysical entities created by humans are astral imps. One of the archaic meanings of the word *imp* is "offspring." Our unhealthy habits and personality patterns may become imps in the Spheres of the Personality/Astral Triad, influencing our thoughts, feelings and actions. That is, little conscious entities or swirls of energy inhabiting the soul in the realms of Yesod in the smaller Trees of the Personality/Astral Triad are the offspring of our habits, will and creative energy that take on a life of their own within the soul. We are responsible for them because we create them, usually unconsciously.

The imps in the Yesod of Hod are made up primarily of coagulated mental astral energy. Those in Netzach are composed mostly of emotional astral energy; and those in Yesod proper are mainly coagulations of vital or etheric astral energy. Imps and other nonphysical entities may inhabit areas connected to the physical human body within a kind of duplicate, nonphysical subtle body—sometimes called the "astral body" or "etheric double" in metaphysical literature.[3] The specific areas they inhabit correspond to the Sephiroth or energy centers out of which they emerge and within which they function. Each Sephira on the Tree of Life corresponds to a particular area of the human body from Crown (the top of the head) to Kingdom (the base of the spine). Perhaps Paul is referring to astral imps in Romans 7:23 where he writes of "the law of sin that lives in my body" or "that dwells in my members."

The idea of nonphysical, unclean spirits inhabiting the human body on the parallel astral or etheric level is implicit in Mark 1:26, where we read, "The unclean spirit, convulsing him and crying out with a loud voice, came out of him," after Jesus commanded it to do so. This healing by Jesus freed the man with the unclean spirit from the spirit's negative influences in his body and mind. The unclean spirit convulsed the man Jesus healed because it was inside his physical body on the corresponding subtle or astral level of Yesod (the animal soul).

Upon leaving the man, the unclean spirit (a creation of impure human desires and habits) would have to roam the shadow lands of Yesod and the animal soul, looking for a new host to inhabit and feed off of. Yesod, on the Central Pillar of the Tree, is, among other things, a parallel universe of astral matter and activity corresponding exactly and connected directly to the physical universe of Malkuth and its contents. These two realms of created reality (astral and physical) are in continuous interaction with each other, so that a change in one of them causes a corresponding change in the other.

All the nonphysical entities in the Personality/Astral Triad are made up of differing grades of coagulated astral energy. Just as the energy of creation takes on increasingly denser qualities of image, form and consciousness in descending the Tree from Crown (Kether) to Kingdom (Malkuth), so does this energy manifest in progressively lighter and more expansive modes of expression as it evolves back up the Tree in accord with the divine plan. When our habit patterns take on a life of their own, like the "autonomous complexes" in Jungian psychology,[4] they also develop a consciousness of their own within the soul and in the astral realms of Yesod.

Our habits are an essential, living part of our personality patterns, reflecting our strengths and weaknesses. By exercising our weaknesses, we strengthen them; and there are astral imps, unclean spirits and demonic entities in the invisible world associated with every type of evil thought and unhealthy addiction. These evil beings, some of which are our own creations, encourage us to pursue our false self's happiness programs and to exercise our weaknesses, so that we will feed them our life-force energy and become increasingly subject to their corrupting influence. This is a battleground of good versus evil in the soul.

The astral impulses or imps of our habit patterns may be communicated from one person to another and sometimes we interact with them in our dreams—which take place in astral realms of the Personality/Astral Triad. Everything we perceive in dreams or visions is made up of varying grades of astral matter in the Spheres of the Personality/Astral Triad. It is real structure and substance, but not as solid or dense as the physical matter in Malkuth seems to be. The reality and malleability of subtle astral matter in the realms of human imagination, the animal soul and the Personality/Astral Triad is a function of humanity's God-given power to create at will, both consciously and unconsciously, and constitutes one of the deeper mysteries of the human soul. This power to create, consciously and unconsciously in the astral realms, and to endow some of our creations with life and consciousness, is one of the important and little known consequences of our being created in the image and likeness of God (Gen. 1:26–27). On our limited microcosmic level in the Personality/Astral Triad, we do what God does on the grand macrocosmic level of the entire Tree of Life.

As little imps or conscious entities living in the soul, our habits feed off of the energy we give them when we repeat their patterns—which we may do by choice consciously or automatically by habit subconsciously. Since our habits are our creations, we're responsible for them and their consequences. Each habit living in the soul has its own innate survival instinct and desire to grow and become stronger. Habits that become addictions and get out of control may become stronger than we are. This is what happens in the case of emotional happiness programs that take over one's life. When we choose not to repeat a habit and are able to not repeat it, we deprive that habit of energy and it will react to this deprivation by complaining and protesting as much as it can in the form of afflictive emotions.

These afflictive emotions will cause us to feel restless, irritated, deprived, empty, angry, lonely, envious, sad, hungry, starved with aching desire and so forth, as the hungry imp of our habit tries to prod us into repeating it again. Hence, an inner struggle ensues as our freedom is challenged by habits of our own making. If we're able, with God's help, to persistently not repeat an unhealthy habit, in spite of the pain and difficulty this costs us, deprived of the energy it needs, that habit will gradually weaken and fade away into unconsciousness with its astral image slumbering in our soul.

Repeatedly choosing to not repeat an unhealthy habit pattern eventually becomes a habit in its own right. As this new counter-habit gradually grows stronger than the habit we want to eliminate, we begin to experience freedom from our addiction to the former habit pattern. This is an essential aspect of how we may do our part to overcome and withdraw from unhealthy addictions of all sorts—that is, physical, emotional, mental, social, and so on—that may run and ruin one's life. This painful struggle is also a spiritual and metaphorical participation in the Paschal Mystery of Jesus on the Cross,[5] a way of dying to our false self that leads to our purification, healing, integration and inner resurrection in the soul.

VI

Permanently changing any of our habit patterns requires not only depriving them of energy to weaken them, but also eliminating the active structural patterns of their images and energy vibrations. Habits in the personality have been described as "magnetic whirls of vibratory patterns" in the soul's energy field.[6] The living structures of these magnetic whirls of energy contain the images, emotions, impulses and desires of our various habit patterns, all composed of moving astral matter in Yesod and the Personality/Astral Triad. Our false self's emotional happiness programs figure prominently among these magnetic energy whirls as dominant patterns. Consequently, dismantling the false-self system requires both depriving its habits of fresh energy and the destruction of its astral images, energy whirls and patterns in the unconscious.

When unhealthy habit patterns of the false self have been deprived of energy and weakened, so they no longer control us, the lingering imprints of those personality patterns still remain alive in the soul—which means they may come back to afflict us. That is, the residue of the false self's happiness programs and afflictive emotions remains alive in the soul and may possibly be recharged, until the active images of the false self's desires and impulses are fully destroyed. Hence, the job of inner purification is not complete until the active astral forms of our unhealthy habits and personality patterns in the unconscious are eliminated by the divine action. Only then may they not be easily resurrected and reactivated when some unexpected temptation presents itself to us in the guise of opportunity under the psychology of seduction: "Look, there it is, you know you want it, go for it!" The memory or imprint of these destroyed patterns will remain in the records of Yesod, but in a non-active, latent state as part of the knowledge gained by both painful and pleasurable experiences.

The destruction and replacement of the false self's habit patterns in the Yesods of the Personality/Astral Triad require the introduction of new energy vibrations and images that are capable of creating constructive change in the soul. The infusion of higher frequency energy vibrations and patterns from the Spiritual/Moral Triad via Tiphareth (Christ in us) into the Personality/Astral Triad and Malkuth (the human personality) is the practical means by which unhealthy personality patterns, habits and addictions may be eliminated and replaced from within. Higher energies of spiritual integration vibrate down through the upper Sephiroth and energy paths of the soul, from Tiphareth, Chesed and Geburah above down into the Personality/Astral Triad. This obviously requires some effective spiritual practices done regularly in humble faith and receptivity; and it requires our willing consent and cooperation with the transformation process—which means doing our part to eliminate unhealthy patterns and to support healthy change and growth in our personality, life and consciousness.

We may wonder what makes this inner transformation process possible: it's possible because all created reality is made up of energy waves existing along an infinite continuum of dimensions and possibilities within the divine consciousness of non-created Reality. The Tree of Life is one comprehensive map representing this continuum of energy waves and the impressions they create in our soul's energy field. Our evolving soul and consciousness, through and within which we experience life and our awareness of existence, are made up of non-physical, high frequency energy-wave vibrations that belong to the universal continuum of created reality within God's consciousness that is absolute oneness and intimacy with everything. The divine consciousness is the master energy pattern, containing and sustaining all lesser patterns within its Self. Hence, it is capable of transforming any and all of these lesser energy patterns at will, in accordance with the workings of its plan.

The divine consciousness is the greater context in which the transformation of each soul and its personality patterns takes place. Given the Tree of Life as a master symbol representing created reality and the divine image reflected in the mirror of time, space and consciousness, each evolving individual soul is a potential microcosmic replica of the living Tree and God's divine image. The actual manifestation of this in each of us is the fulfillment of the divine plan. Toward this end, we are invited to take up the work of becoming our true self by living and growing in harmony with God's will and plan for us, which is the perfect plan for our greatest good and ultimate fulfillment. Following this path, however we may do so, is the practice of true religion and true spirituality.

The alignment of the habits and patterns in our human personality with the divine will is an essential part of this process, a necessary prerequisite for its completion. Toward this end, subtle vibrations from above may descend the Tree of Life to renew our patterns of self-creation in the Personality/Astral Triad. This is the benevolent work of the Spirit in the soul and it's the inner work of Centering Prayer. It's the work of our soul in partnership with Christ to become our true self. More details of this inner renewal process involving Centering Prayer and the divine action in us are discussed in the next chapter.

10

THE INNER WORK OF CENTERING PRAYER

I

Centering Prayer is a very subtle spiritual practice: a gentle, non-conceptual movement into the simplicity of the present moment. The working basis of Centering Prayer is an inner attitude of consent to God's presence and action in us and in our life. The simple repetition of a sacred symbol (word, gaze or breath) is used to affirm our intention to consent; and it's used to help us avoid possible distractions until, by God's grace, our mind is quiet and we silently, effortlessly rest in our consent to the divine presence and action within. What could be simpler than saying "Yes" to our relationship with God and God's will for us by accepting reality just as it is, right now?

This may be simple in principle but it's not always easy in practice, especially when we don't like what we're experiencing in the present moment. Learning non-judgmental patience and expectation-free acceptance of whatever's happening in our consciousness during the time of Centering Prayer, as being God's will for us in the moment, is an essential part of the discipline of Centering Prayer. This discipline calls for humility, faith and commitment to the simple, uncomplicated process of the prayer, which helps these inner attitudes to grow in us; and it calls for returning to our sacred symbol as needed to maintain our intention.

The regular daily practice of Centering Prayer is a practical means for initiating, sustaining and cooperating with the processes of inner purification, healing and transformation on the deepest, most secret level of our being. This discipline is a humble way of exercising our relationship with God in partnership with Christ. It allows us to touch base with our inner depths and to grow in self-knowledge.

Two periods of Centering Prayer each day for a minimum of twenty minutes each are recommended. Thomas Keating has said that what's required for the inner work of Centering Prayer to move forward is simply to be faithful to our regular daily practice of this prayer and consenting to be transformed by the divine action. The rest is up to God, i.e., Father, Son and Holy Spirit working in our soul. This assumes, of course, that we're living a life of prayer, worship and action based on the gospel values taught by Jesus while living in harmony with conscience as best we can.

How we live our life in the world and in relation to others is the outer work of Centering Prayer. This outer work has a direct bearing on Centering Prayer's inner work and our inner relationship with Christ. It involves working to improve our self while humbly accepting our whole self as we actually are. This requires willingness to know the truth about our self, especially our false self; and it requires willingness to change. It challenges us to do all we can to cooperate with the divine action by working to eliminate unhealthy habits of thought, feeling, speech and action, and to live the gospel values in daily life. Giving love, truth and freedom to others to whatever degree we can, and working with some outer spiritual practices, such as those taught by Contemplative Outreach, e.g., Lectio Divina, using an active prayer sentence and the Welcoming Prayer,[1] are some practical ways of doing our part to cooperate with the divine action in our life.

How may we give love, truth and freedom to others? Accepting others as they are and respecting their legitimate rights and needs are fundamental to living in harmony with our conscience. We may give love to others by caring, being compassionate and honoring their intrinsic preciousness as spiritual beings. We may give truth through honesty and integrity in our dealings with others; and we may give freedom to others by allowing and encouraging them to be who they are and to make their own choices. This is basic spirituality on the level of human relationships. There are, of course, false-self obstacles in us that make practicing such spirituality in our life and relations with others difficult and challenging at times.

Another practice we may use for supporting our relationship with God and keeping our peace in tact in daily life involves four different outer attitudes and the single inner attitude of benevolence and love toward everyone. The single inner attitude is based on the spiritual truth that we are all one in Christ's love on the deepest level. The four outer attitudes we express toward others correspond to four different ways in which they may be feeling and acting as we encounter them in the present moment. The first of these is the person who is feeling happy and enjoying life. The appropriate way to act outwardly toward such a person is to be happy with them that they're happy while inwardly loving them in Christ. The second example is the person who's unhappy, who is suffering pain and sadness. The appropriate outward behavior toward such a person is to have compassion and help them if we can while inwardly loving and identifying with them.

The third type of person is the one who is doing virtuous behavior, showing integrity and living the gospel values. We are to give joy and honor to such people who are upholding righteousness and the spiritual values of integrity and honesty, mercy and kindness. It's easy to love and admire such individuals because they're doing what we know is right.

The fourth way an individual may behave outwardly is to exhibit negative or evil behavior that violates the legitimate rights, needs and intrinsic value of one's self, others, or God's creation. When faced with dishonest, corrupt, harmful or perverse behavior, we need to make a choice: for example, we may expose, confront and resist the evil behavior; allow, condone or take part in it; or we may take an outwardly detached, neutral attitude toward it, as if ignoring it, getting away from the negative person if we can while secretly holding love and compassion in our heart for her or him.[2] Jesus encourages this inner attitude toward our adversaries in Matthew 5:44 saying, "Love your enemies and pray for those who persecute you." This latter course of action is not easy to do, for obvious reasons, but is the one recommended if we wish to truly follow the gospel and keep inner peace intact. However, we need to evaluate each situation on a case-by-case basis and decide which course of outward action is appropriate for being true to oneself, cooperating with the divine action and doing the outer work of Centering Prayer—which may call for patience, forgiveness, self-control and letting-go of pride and ego. Or it may call for openly confronting and trying to correct something that's wrong.[3]

II

The outer work of Centering Prayer supports its inner work, and vice versa. Centering Prayer's inner work is simple and subtle. It's God's work in us supported by our willing consent and cooperation. The real work of Centering Prayer is not something we do but something God does in us to the degree we allow it by the sincerity and depth of our consent. The false self in our soul does not want to consent and allow this work of the divine action in us. This is why we begin Centering Prayer with the conscious *intention* of consenting to the divine action. If we could actually consent, fully and freely, consciously and unconsciously, then we'd have no false self and we'd already be living in the fullness of divine union; and we'd be able to freely enjoy practicing the gospel values of love and forgiveness toward everyone, at least inwardly in our heart.

As love, truth and freedom are primary spiritual values, the Lord has given us free will, allowing us to say "Yes" or "No" to what's offered as we're all invited into a deepening relationship of communion and union, intimacy and oneness with God; that is, we're free to say "Yes" or "No" to this divine invitation. It's our willing consent, our saying "Yes" to love and its commitment to the other that makes love real and meaningful. This is a two-way relationship, freely chosen and entered into by both parties or all parties involved. It can work only if all parties involved will do their part in supporting and sustaining the relationship.

If it's not freely chosen and entered into, then it's not true love—which means willingly surrendering and freely giving one's self to the beloved other. This has to be a mutual self-surrender and is exactly what God longs to do in relation to each of us; that is, to freely surrender and give God's Self to us in the miraculous holy mystery of divine love, truth and freedom. The purpose of the inner work of Centering Prayer is to prepare us to receive this greatest of gifts— which is the gift of the Holy Spirit, the gift of our life in Christ, and the "reward" of divine union with the Father (Matthew 6:6). We may come to know or understand what this gift actually is only to the degree that we receive it; and in receiving it, we move through the progressive stages of our soul's rebirth in Christ. As a simple means to accessing the gift of non-conceptual, apophatic contemplation, Centering Prayer is totally in the service of our rebirth in Christ.

God's will for us is to make us into a unique new creation in the divine image of our true self, as Paul writes of in 2 Corinthians 5:17. This marvelous work of Christ and the Spirit in us is fulfilled through the gift of silent contemplation; that is, through the full development of God's presence and action alive in us. There is, in each person, an inner center of peace, strength and wisdom, a place of truth, beauty and goodness that manifests the soul's inner wealth. The aim of Centering Prayer is to bring us, through the gift of contemplation, into this True Center of our being—which is our divine inheritance. In the loving process of this inner journey, we give our whole self, including our false self, to God: and God gives our true self and God's Self to us in return; so we may receive our treasure of divine inheritance. This is a most wonderful and profitable exchange of gifts all around, inspired and sustained by the goodness of divine love—our life in Christ's Mystical Body.

The fulfillment of God's plan in us is the greatest of "win-win" outcomes where we lose our false self and gain the greatest of gifts— our true self of divine inheritance. In this blessed exchange of spiritual energies, God's will and plan are brought to fruition in us as love increases to share more and more of its eternal goodness in created reality. To accomplish this victory, the ground of love's growth in us must be prepared for planting, cultivation and harvest. Human nature is the ground for our spiritual growth and the outer and inner works of Centering Prayer are the labors of its preparation, cultivation and ultimate harvest in Christ (Tiphareth) in the center of our soul on the Tree of Life.

III

Centering Prayer prepares us for the gift of contemplation. In consenting to God's presence and action, we give the Spirit permission to enter the living structures of our habits and personality patterns in the Spheres of the Personality/Astral Triad so the divine action may work our inner purification, healing and transformation. As in human relationships that produce changes in us, our inner relationship with God in prayer is an energy exchange that powerfully and profoundly affects the state of our soul. Humility and faith are the basis of our receptive capacity in relation to God, and the sincerity and depth of our consent to the divine action determine the levels of soul on which we're actually open and willing to receive the divine energy and influence.

The practical results of Centering Prayer—that is, the fruits that show up in daily life—depend in no small measure on our willingness to allow the Spirit to do its work in us; for the Spirit respects our free will and works in concert with it. Thus, the sincerity and depth of our consent to the divine action and doing our part to cooperate with it are essential determining factors in Centering Prayer. To begin with, we're generally not able to fully consent to the divine action as we aspire to because of unconscious resistance and our false-self tendencies. However, our conscious intention to consent opens the door for the Spirit's redemptive work to begin in us, in the unconscious recesses of Yesod/Foundation.

As we continue faithfully in daily practice of Centering Prayer, our intention to consent grows stronger and becomes a new habit. This new habit of intending to consent is nourished by regular practice and by the energy of God's grace infused into the soul. As our intention to consent grows stronger, our ability to actually consent increases, in spite of resistance from counter habits and the false self. The process of our inner purification, healing and rebirth in Christ takes time because it takes time for the habits of our conscious and unconscious attitudes, will and desires to come into alignment with God's will in us.

How do our personality patterns and habits of attitude, will and desire get changed? This is an important question with both outer and inner answers. Outwardly, we need to identify our personal habits and patterns, evaluate them, and work to withdraw from those that are unhealthy and contrary to spiritual growth, as discussed in previous chapters. This will serve to weaken our false-self patterns by depriving them of energy. We also need to consciously cultivate healthy counter-habits that support our human health and spiritual growth. Inwardly, there's a healing and transformation process carried on in secret by the Spirit in conjunction with our daily Centering Prayer practice. This hidden process is what we're calling "the inner work of Centering Prayer." It involves inner energy exchanges with the divine presence and action that engender changes in us in the direction of God's plan for us, i.e., in the direction of becoming our true self.

Every relationship is an energy exchange. Let's take a brief look at human energy exchanges as an example: The human soul is a multi-dimensional energy field that extends well beyond the physical body in Malkuth. Whenever two or more individuals interact, their energy fields overlap and interpenetrate, creating an exchange of information and energies among them. This is a natural, inevitable process of interpersonal contact and it's an important part of how we influence one another. Exchanging subtle energies with others on levels of the Personality/Astral-Triad Spheres can be a kind of silent ministry, a way of spreading goodwill and bringing Christ into the world, if we choose to do so. Energy exchanges with others may be positive, negative or neutral, depending on our level of receptivity and the quality of energies involved.

It works like this: when two or more individuals come into contact, their energy fields blend and an exchange takes place on certain levels of the Personality/Astral Triad and, in some cases, on levels of the Spiritual/Moral Triad as well. The energy each one receives has an effect that creates change in her or his energy field. When the individuals separate, some of the energy they've received remains in each one's energy field and some of the energy they've shared remains in the energy field of the other or others.

Energy exchanges with others are always stimulating to some degree, since they introduce new vibrations into one's energy field. The energies we receive from others may be nourishing or toxic, inspiring or depressing, exciting or calming, etc. They may stimulate the best or the worst in us. Or they may be relatively flat and neutral. The point is they do affect us and we can usually determine the quality of the energy we receive from another by how we feel while we're with that person as well as after we've been with them. We're responsible for the energies we give to others through interacting with them.

Some people are primarily givers of energy and others are takers. There's always some give and take in any energy exchange. The net result determines how we feel about spending time with that person. We may feel positive, negative or neutral, attracted, repelled or indifferent. The experience depends on how the energy fields of two or more souls blend together, which may be harmonious or inharmonious, etc. There apparently is an infinite variety of combinations and mixtures of energy fields possible. Sometimes the effects are quite obvious, but often energy exchanges with others are subtle and multilayered.

When we pray and relate to God, we have an inner energy exchange with the divine presence. The nature and depth of our energy exchange with God is very subtle and depends on how we're relating to God; that is, our levels of faith and humility, sincerity and reverence, devotion and gratitude, willingness to listen and respond to silent urgings of the Spirit. It depends on the extent to which we're relating to God out of our false self versus our true self. On the deepest level, we simply need to consent and surrender to the divine action. This will bring us into the deepest and fullest energy exchange with God, opening us to the gift of pure contemplation. The inner work of Centering Prayer gradually brings us to the point where we're capable of fully consenting and surrendering to the divine action and love of Christ in us.

The energy we receive from the Spirit during Centering Prayer engenders positive change in our soul. As we consent to the divine action, a pathway on the Middle Pillar of the Tree of Life in us opens and Christ, the redeemer, descends from Tiphareth in the Spiritual/ Moral Triad down into Yesod, the place of patterns in the Personality/Astral Triad. Silencing the functions of memory, intellect and imagination in the Spheres of the Personality/Astral Triad, the divine action enters Yesod in the small Trees of the Personality/Astral

Sephiroth (Yesod, Hod and Netzach), infusing new energies of higher frequencies into the living structures of astral matter that constitute the personality's habit patterns of thought, feeling, action, attitude, will and desire.

The higher-frequency energies of the divine action adapt themselves and match-up to the patterns and frequencies of the astral-matter structures of our habits and personality patterns. Those habits and personality patterns that are in harmony with the divine action are supported. Those which are contrary to it are attacked and dismantled as follows: Vibrating in unison with the astral-matter structures of the false self's habits and patterns in the unconscious (Yesod), the master energy pattern of the divine action accelerates their frequencies to the point where their structural integrity breaks down and they shatter into pieces. This destructive process is analogous to how a sustained high-pitch note sung by a trained opera singer can shatter into pieces the crystal structure of an empty wine glass. The vibratory destruction of false-self personality patterns is the final phase in their permanent elimination and may come about only after they've been drained of energy by persistent non-repetition, i.e., only after the habit has been broken and, like an empty wine glass, its form has no energy inside to support and hold it together.

IV

The energy we receive from the Spirit during Centering Prayer engenders change in our soul as we grow in consent toward full surrender or union of wills with God. As we progress in the outer work of Centering Prayer, withdrawing from unhealthy habits of thought, feeling and action, replacing them with healthy habits, and as the sincerity and depth of our consent to the divine action increase, the Spirit is able to work more profoundly in concert with our will. This leads to the final destruction of the false self's habit and personality patterns, the toxic residue of which is recycled into non-created Reality via the Qlippoth at the bottom of the small Trees in the Personality/Astral Triad. Some of this residue may be experienced as unloading of the unconscious.

Destruction of the false self's patterns also leads to the creation of new personality and habit patterns that express the true self through the fruits and gifts of the Spirit.[4] This is the inner resurrection of our life in Christ that accompanies the death of our false self. It is the spiritual victory of our rebirth in Christ.

The death of the false self and birth of the new self generally happen simultaneously by gradual steps or degrees, sometimes imperceptibly to our day-to-day consciousness. There's often an alternation between unloading the unconscious—the inner purification process—and the gentle discovery of our new consciousness in God's humble, loving presence. Sometimes it feels like we're progressing in the journey; other times it seems we're regressing and getting worse as the unconscious unloads its toxic contents of unhealed wounds, afflictive emotions and immature habit patterns. We feel less integrated and together as the Nights of Sense and Spirit temporarily engulf us.[5] Following the desolations of unloading, we may feel consoled, healed or reassured by the grace of God's silent presence. There may be an alternation between these two types of experiences for some time, until the process finally works itself out; and when that's completed, only God knows. When we begin to live in an abiding sense of God's presence, no matter what happens, that's a good sign that we're getting free of the false self. As obstacles are removed by the divine action, our growing freedom to consent more fully and deeply becomes cause for increasing peace and joy in the soul. This is a gift of divine love.

Each person's conscious experience of the spiritual journey and inner work of Centering Prayer is different, as the Spirit works with each of us individually, according to each soul's particular needs, unique psycho-spiritual condition and personal temperament. In some cases, the unloading and transformation processes are experienced vividly on a conscious level. In other instances, they take place mostly unconsciously. In his book, *Invitation to Love*, Thomas Keating discusses the idea of "lights-on" and "lights-off" mysticism, which he credits to Ruth Burrows in her book, *Guidelines for Mystical Prayer*. In lights-on mysticism, a person has a variety of experiences of the felt presence of God and mystical phenomena, such as visions, voices, consolations, energy currents in the chakras (Sephiroth) and subtle body, and even physical levitation—which Teresa of Avila is known to have experienced.

In lights-off mysticism, there are no such phenomena or felt experiences of God's presence. The spiritual journey is relatively dry and uneventful, in terms of mystical phenomena, emotional consolations and so forth. This is what John of the Cross has called "the path of pure faith," which he considers to be "the proximate means of union with God." This path does not depend on flashy experiences or emotional consolations, but plods faithfully along, resting in an inner conviction and trust in God's abiding benevolence, presence and mercy. It's a more mature and markedly less sensational spirituality than lights-on mysticism. Centering Prayer with lights-off mysticism is more completely "prayer in secret," since the inner work and movements of the prayer remain almost entirely unconscious.

Each of these two contrasting paths leads to the same divine union. So we cannot say that one is better than the other. What we can do is trust that the Lord will give us the path that is right for us. For many spiritual seekers and Centering Prayer practitioners, much of the time, it's lights-off mysticism—which can save one from some distractions and temptations to spiritual pride, though not all of them. For most of us, the spiritual journey will be some relative combination of lights-off and lights-on mysticism—as God wills for us. In all cases, consenting and submitting to the process of inner purification and healing in trust and cooperation with the divine action are essential for the inner work of Centering Prayer to move forward. This inner work is God's great gift to us—the "reward" from "the Father who sees in secret" Jesus mentions in Matthew 6:6.

V

Two essential aspects of Centering Prayer's inner work are: 1) the unloading process that accompanies inner healing and death of the false self and 2) building up the new self. Thomas Keating has discussed the unloading of the unconscious extensively in his books and recorded talks.[6] In terms of the Tree of Life and the four Sephiroth of the human personality, Netzach, Hod, Yesod and Malkuth, the unloading process is experienced as thoughts in Hod, emotions in Netzach, memories and animal passions in Yesod, and a variety of bodily sensations in Malkuth.

Unloading is precipitated as the astral structures of the false-self system are broken down, unresolved emotions and conflicting thoughts are evacuated, old memories surface, energy blockages in the body are released, and the residue of the inner healing process passes out through consciousness. Unloading may also be triggered by external events, people, relationships, expectations, fears, stress, etc. God often uses conspiracies of coincidence and circumstance in our outer life to effect changes in our inner life. How people experience the unloading process differs from one person to another and depends particularly on what's within them that needs healing. Combining the idea of lights-on and lights-off mysticism with the concept of unloading the unconscious, we may speak of lights-on and lights-off unloading occurring in different individuals and at different times in the same individual. In other words, unloading may occur consciously (lights-on) or unconsciously (lights-off).

Lights-on unloading may involve a repeating pattern where consoling, inspiring and reassuring experiences are followed by discouraging experiences of humiliating self-knowledge, intense negative affect and feeling alienated from God. Lights-off unloading is much less dramatic and characterized by depressing feelings of dullness, dryness and boredom without any felt reassurances of God's love beforehand. One may feel low on energy, restless or empty inside. Unloading may involve warring passions in the animal soul (Yesod); confused, conflicting thoughts in Hod; disordered emotions and desires in Netzach; and a variety of unpleasant symptoms in the physical body (Malkuth). All these things stem from unresolved earlier life experiences that were repressed, as well as from impure imps or spirits we've contacted or created through our false-self desires, habits and personality patterns.

As mentioned earlier, the disintegration and dying of the false self occurs as its core habit and personality patterns are destroyed by the withholding of energy and by vibratory destruction of their living images and patterns in the astral matter of the unconscious (Yesod). Like the false pagan gods of prehistory and antiquity, which were (are) collective super-imps or thought-forms created by the group-consciousness and worship of various peoples, our humanly created habit patterns and astral imps cannot continue to live and grow unless we feed them with the vital energy of our will, worship, ritual behaviors and sacrifices, i.e., with our dedicated thoughts, feelings and actions. If we withdraw our support, they're deprived of energy and wither away. God does not support them from within as we are supported because they are not God's creations; they are our creations. Hence, they're dependent on our energy and, as centers of consciousness or entities inhabiting our souls and the astral realms of Yesod, they greatly fear starvation.

Once weakened by starvation, the astral shells or forms of our false-self habits and personality patterns, no longer sustained by the energy of our will, are easily broken apart and disintegrated by the higher-frequency energy vibrations of the divine action working in us. The imprints of their images remain in the memory records of Yesod as learning experiences, but they're no longer active or able to be revived as living forces of motivation—unless we deliberately choose to re-create them, which would mean rejecting our spiritual growth and regressing back to earlier modes of functioning.

The disruption and disintegration of our unhealthy personality patterns, which include our unhealed wounds and emotional reactions to them, inevitably precipitate the unloading process. Though it may feel quite negative at times, this unloading is actually a gift and positive sign that we are experiencing an opportunity and challenge for real healing and growth. The results, of course, always depend on how we choose to respond to this unloading: by accepting and welcoming it in good faith, or by resisting, rejecting and suppressing it via rationalizations and justifications of the false self and its ego-defense mechanisms.

VI

The complementary process to unloading the unconscious and eliminating the false-self system's patterns is creation of the new self and healthy patterns to replace them. This renewal process yields a new integration and wholeness of the personality with the gospel values growing in us, fruits and gifts of the Spirit emerging in daily life, and habits of thought, feeling and action that support and express our true self. As the false-self system weakens out and declines, the new self grows stronger and arises more frequently into consciousness.

There comes about a gradual shifting of our center of identity from the false self to the true self. We learn to regard our human personality as a vehicle or instrument we use for functioning in the world rather than as our center and source of identity. By God's grace, we gradually discover the true center and source of our identity to be the divine indwelling of Christ in Tiphareth and the Spiritual/Moral Triad within us.

The destruction of the false self and the building of our true self in the Personality/Astral Triad—the spiritual refinement of our personality—tend to go on simultaneously. As old habit patterns of the false self are drained of energy and broken down, they're replaced by the creation of new habits and patterns in the Spheres of the Personality/Astral Triad. The result of this rebirth process is the emergence of a new dimension of consciousness in our daily life in Malkuth. This new-consciousness dimension is grounded in the subtle awareness of God's abiding presence within and around us. This is the "hidden treasure" and "pearl of great value" Jesus speaks of in Matthew 13:44–46.

The recurring alternations between various types of unloading episodes and temporary experiences of spiritual awakening correlate to the destruction of the false self's habit patterns and the building of the new self through the inner work of Centering Prayer—at least in instances of lights-on mysticism where what's happening in the unconscious (Yesod) shows up as definite signs of unloading and spiritual growth in one's waking consciousness. All of this is the work of the divine action in us.

Centering Prayer's practice of consenting to the divine action gives permission for the process of this inner work to go on in us. The inner absorption of deep rest that's eventually brought about during Centering Prayer is central in this hidden process. When the faculties of intellect (Hod), imagination (Netzach) and memory (Yesod) are suspended by the divine action, and when the battle between good and evil in the soul is relatively resolved, so that the personality is at peace and in harmony with true conscience in Geburah, then the inner work of rebirth in Christ moves forward unhindered.

One of the requirements of our spiritual conscience, inspired by the universal love and benevolence of Chesed / Mercy, and expressed in a core teaching of Jesus, is that we forgive everyone who has angered, hurt or offended us. The process of doing so is true Christian practice and incumbent on every faithful follower of Jesus.[7] The peace of this release promotes healing and rest in the soul, and helps open us to receive the precious gifts of contemplation and spiritual inheritance.

In Ezekiel 36:23–26, we read: "'When I prove my holiness among you, I will gather you from all foreign lands; and I will pour clean water upon you and cleanse you from all your impurities, and I will give you a new spirit,' says the Lord."

When we discover the Lord's holiness, we dedicate ourselves to the spiritual journey; then, the Lord gathers us together by bringing to light the personality's fragmented parts that are lost in "foreign lands." This scripture passage describes allegorically what happens in the soul through the inner work of Centering Prayer and the gift of silent contemplation.

11

THE MYSTERY OF DAATH / THE CLOUD

I

Daath/the Cloud and its relation to Centering Prayer have been introduced in the second half of chapter 6; the reader may find it helpful to review those pages. As previously mentioned, Daath/the Cloud is the dark, invisible Sphere that cannot be conceived by the intellect. It is utterly apophatic (without images) and identified with the Great Abyss separating the top of the Spiritual/Moral Triad, Chesed/Mercy, from the bottom of the Supernal Triad, Binah/Understanding. On the Universal Tree of Life, Daath is the portal of passage from individual consciousness into the Spheres of universal consciousness in the Supernal Triad. It's also the evolutionary link of consciousness transformations connecting the smaller Trees of Life existing within the Ten Sephiroth of the individual soul's energy field or microcosmic Tree, as will be explained below.

The symbol of the Cloud appears in both the Torah and the New Testament as a manifestation of God's presence in Malkuth. For example, the Israelites were led by a cloud while wandering in the desert. When "the cloud covered the tent of meeting, the glory of the Lord filled the tabernacle.... Whenever the cloud was taken up from the tabernacle, the Israelites would set out on each stage of their journey..., and fire was in the cloud by night" (Ex. 40:34–38). In Exodus 34:5, God speaks to Moses out of a cloud; and an awesome cloud overshadows Moses, Elijah, Jesus and the three disciples, Peter, James and John, on Mount Tabor at the time of the Transfiguration

(Luke 9:28–35). The voice from this cloud says of Jesus, "This is my beloved Son, listen to him."

All of these scripture passages have profound allegorical implications for the practice of contemplative prayer, e.g., the glory of the Lord filling the tabernacle suggests the awakening of the divine indwelling in the soul's inner tabernacle or deepest center, with Daath/the Cloud enfolding it. Elijah, who appeared with Moses conversing with Jesus on Mount Tabor, has been called "the patron of contemplative prayer," since he experienced the Lord God passing by his cave as "sheer silence" on the holy mountain (1 Kings 19:11–13). This signaled a new way for God to relate to humans, and for us to relate to God: the quiet listening way of apophatic contemplation. Inner listening in receptive silence is the basic disposition of the contemplation into which Centering Prayer gradually leads us, as the Lord wills. Also, in *The Cloud of Unknowing*, the anonymous fourteenth-century manual for contemplative prayer upon which the method of Centering Prayer is based, the divine presence is indicated as an inner heavenly cloud into which the soul's receptive consciousness enters.

Inner silence is the portal of entry into Daath/the Cloud. Silence means relaxing into the present moment and letting-go or detaching from any thoughts, images, emotions, bodily sensations, urges, stimulations or particular perceptions that may arise in consciousness. Silence is a state of non-doing brought about in us by the grace and divine action of the Spirit. As silence deepens, we move into deeper levels of listening, entering a mysterious state of open, empty consciousness without an object, a state of inner absorption, peace and rest that's calm and still. It's not a state of unconsciousness because we know we're somewhere when we're in it, but we don't know where we are other than simply here and now in this deep inner space beyond time and place. These words are kataphatic hints or suggestions pointing toward the soul's ineffable entry into apophatic contemplation—which is a timeless state of profound rest, peace and invisible silence—a gift received when the faculties are quiet and still; that is, when the physical body (Malkuth) is at peace and the activities of the Personality/Astral-Triad Sephiroth are suspended by the finer frequencies of created reality's master energy pattern working silently and secretly in us. In this state of profound inner calm, the Spirit does some of its deepest work in us, in secret.

It's the divine action itself that quiets our mind in appropriate moments and brings us to rest in Daath/the Cloud. As we rest there in empty silence, consenting to the Spirit's presence and action, God goes to work as needed in the other Spheres of our soul. God goes to work in the smaller Trees within the individual Sephiroth, especially in Yesod (the Sephira of memories and patterns), and in the larger Sephiroth themselves. In most cases, this all takes place in secret, as the Spirit plumbs our soul's unconscious depths. Inner purification, healing and unloading the unconscious are natural byproducts of this process, which goes on secretly as we simply rest in silence, consenting to God's will—which may also work in us when our mind is not so quiet.

There are three, nonphysical, invisible Walls encountered and penetrated by consciousness in the deepening processes of contemplative prayer or meditation. These are the inner Walls of Thoughts, Energy and Silence. The energy manifesting created reality arises from silence, and thoughts arise from this energy as it is focused and organized into patterns, images and forms of increasing density and complexity moving down the Tree of Life. In Centering Prayer, thoughts include all the particular perceptions we experience in both the inner and outer worlds. Thoughts may be physical, vital, emotional, mental, psychic, social or spiritual. In other words, thoughts are all kataphatic and include much more than thinking. Thoughts are most commonly experienced by humans in the Spheres of Malkuth/Kingdom and the Personality/Astral Triad, though they may also enter human consciousness from higher Spheres of the Spiritual/Moral Triad. The entire Tree of Life and unfolding drama of created reality is a superthought in the divine Absolute Consciousness of God, the Creator manifesting through the Supernal Triad of the Universal Tree and in all individual Trees or souls.

The Wall of Thoughts occupies human consciousness most of the time. Concentrative spiritual practices of meditation, prayer and ritual are kataphatic ways of working with the Wall of Thoughts to contact spiritual energies and awaken the soul's inner life. There's a wide variety of kataphatic practices in the world's religious and spiritual traditions. Some of these are outer practices of verbal prayer, recitation, ritual and righteous action, while others are inner practices of concentrative prayer, visualization and meditation. All of these have their legitimate times, places and roles to play in the spiritual life and development of human souls. Some inner practices of kataphatic prayer and meditation open up into deeper mysteries of the soul's energy field and inner life, moving from the Wall of Thoughts into the Wall of Energy; and some outer practices of ritual, dance and worship, especially ones using music and archetypal images, may move the emotions and also open one to the Wall of Energy, which is the Wall of lights-on experiences.

The Wall of Energy is subtle, underlying the Wall of Thoughts in both inner and outer worlds. This Wall has many layers or dimensions. It's been said that "energy follows thought." This is true, but it's also true that thought arises out of energy. This may be the energy of will, desire, intellect or instinct; that is, it may be energy deriving from Netzach (the Sphere of emotions, will, desire and imagination); energy deriving from Hod (the Sphere of intellect); or energy arising in Yesod (the Sphere of memory, instinct, reproduction, subconsciousness and the animal soul). Energies emanating down the Tree from the Spiritual/Moral Triad may also give rise to thoughts containing higher inspirations, ideals and intuitive insights. The Wall of Energy links everything in created reality together. It interpenetrates and runs through the physical human body, underlying its functioning and animating the soul on all levels as a multidimensional energy field. The Wall of Silence lies within or beneath the Walls of Thoughts and Energy, in timeless, open stillness.

Some concentrative practices of kataphatic prayer and meditation use thoughts, sounds, gestures and images to work with the Wall of Energy, activating and focusing energy currents and flow in the soul's subtle body and energy centers or chakras—also called "Sephiroth" or "the inner holy planets" on the Tree of Life.[1] The Middle Pillar on the Tree correlates to the spinal column and brain in the human body and is the locus of the soul's seven central energy centers or chakras (as explained in endnote 1). These subtle energy centers, along with

Hod and Netzach on the Pillars of Severity and Mercy, produce and house the living structures of our habits and personality patterns in human ground.

Everything in the soul's multi-dimensional energy field is inter-related, from thoughts to energy to the motivation that moves us. Underneath the Wall of Energy and the images it produces is the more subtle Wall of Silence, which opens into Daath/the Cloud. All kata-phatic methods of true mystical prayer and meditation are practical means of spiritual growth that ultimately end in silence.[2] These prac-tices help us relate more directly to God and serve to prepare us for apophatic prayer and meditation in deepening silence, the most pro-found of the profound. This silence brings us repeatedly beyond what we've previously known and, through Daath/the Cloud, into new ter-ritory on the Tree of Life. Ultimately, as we reach the summit of the Tree within us, the soul's passages through Daath/the Cloud bring us beyond individual consciousness into the awesome place of creation's mysterious beginnings in the Supernal Triad and the inconceivable Unity Consciousness of Kether/the Crown.

II

The mystery of Daath/the Cloud, which is unknowable in itself, expresses in us as the place of inner passage from one stage of con-sciousness evolution into the next. It's always a passage of uncertainty beyond words, images and ideas where one's familiar sense of reality is challenged and deconstructed in order to make way for a new foun-dation and beginning; that is, for a restructuring of consciousness. This process is symbolized outwardly in Exodus 13:21 by the cloud and pillar of fire leading the Israelites (God's people) in their passage through the desert (the place of transition and inner dryness) after escaping from the bondage of slavery in Egypt (the place of emotional dependency and addiction to false-self happiness programs). Their goal, of course, is the freedom and prosperity of a new life in the Promised Land into which the Lord God promises to lead them, if they'll keep faith with his covenant as given through Moses. As the story unfolds, they continue clinging to the idols, attitudes and gods of the false-self patterns of other tribes around them that they also carry within them.

In clinging to the old rather than embracing the new, they unfortunately fail to do what God asks of them. In other words, failing to forsake the limitations and errors of their former worldview, values and way of life, the Israelites do not successfully negotiate their passage through Daath into the new level of consciousness that's offered them by the divine action working through Moses—who allegorically represents the inner guidance and wisdom of our conscience and true self urging us to leave our familiar land of Egypt and journey to the Promised Land of our divine inheritance. There's an important lesson in this for all of us. It concerns our need to keep faith with God by trusting the divine action in our self and our life, and to follow through in our partnership with Christ by fully doing our part.

The soul's successive passages through Daath lead to increasing integration and wholeness as we grow toward spiritual maturity on the Tree of Life. Daath in each Sephira is a passageway and threshold into the energies and functions of the Supernal Triad in the smaller Tree within that Sephira. One of the chief functions of the Supernal Triad within the smaller Trees is to universalize consciousness within each Sephira and then, through Kether, to take it to the next level; that is, into the Malkuth at the bottom of the smaller Tree within the next higher Sephira in the soul's microcosmic Tree. To reach its own highest state of consciousness at the peak of its own Kether/Crown, each soul must climb the Tree of Life within itself ten times; that is, it must climb the Tree once in each of its ten visible Sephiroth. It's also been said that an individual soul must do this on the Tree of Life in each of the Four Qabalistic Worlds[3] in order to climb the Universal Tree of the Macrocosm. In any case, we may regard reaching Kether on the Universal Tree as the ultimate term or final goal of an individual soul's consciousness evolution and return to its non-created Source.

As a soul's consciousness ascends its inner Tree of Life, each coming apart of its self-organization or ego-identity in the perilous passages through Daath leads it into a new unification or coming together of its consciousness and energies on a higher level. This continuing deconstruction/reconstruction process is how we climb the ladder of lights within us known as the Tree of Life; that is, step by step. It's a repeating process of death and rebirth, disintegration and reintegration into new levels of consciousness that both contain and supersede all former levels so that nothing of value is lost in the Tree's ascent. In this restructuring of consciousness on the Tree, the false self's limitations of ignorance and immaturity are outgrown but not forgotten as lessons learned and wisdom gained in the game of life. Beyond the preliminary purification of the false-self system in the Personality/Astral Triad, we enter into the divine life of our rebirth in Christ in the Spiritual/Moral Triad.

The Tree of Life is alive in each of us in a unique way. As human beings, we are all developing and functioning in the Spheres of Malkuth and the Personality/Astral Triad simultaneously all the time. The Wall of Thoughts figures prominently in human consciousness in Malkuth and the Personality/Astral Triad. It includes all of our sensory experiences, images, ideals, beliefs, instinctual drives, happiness programs, memories, desires, emotions, dreams and other particular perceptions. The Wall of Energy, which underlies the Wall of Thoughts, is secondary to it in the normal consciousness of the Personality/Astral Triad. In the Spiritual/Moral Triad, where energies are finer and forms less dense, the Wall of Energy is primary and the Wall of Thoughts secondary. In lights-off mysticism, there is minimal experience of the Wall of Energy in Malkuth and the Personality/Astral Triad. In lights-on mysticism there tends to be a lot of conscious experience of the Wall of Energy on all levels. This distinction is fundamental to the difference between these two modes of mystical and contemplative experience, which may function at different times in different people.

In Centering Prayer's lights-off mysticism, passages through Daath/the Cloud in Malkuth and the Spheres of the Personality/Astral Triad are experienced mostly unconsciously, in the soul's secret recesses beneath surface consciousness. One simply does the prayer, rests in silence, experiences symptoms of unloading, feels bored, persecuted by thoughts or maybe thinks that nothing is happening. There may be much returning to the sacred symbol (word, breath or gaze) to avoid distractions and maintain one's intention to consent. Meanwhile, beneath surface awareness in the unconscious, the prayer is working because a lot is actually happening in secret, in the darkness of Malkuth and the Personality/Astral-Triad Sephiroth.

The divine action is always at work in us during Centering Prayer, in accord with the sincerity and depth of our consent, and in subtle ways we may not perceive. Remaining faithful to our daily prayer and consistently consenting to be transformed by the divine action carry us invisibly through the passages of change in the hidden unconscious. The Spirit keeps working in us as long as we consent. As we unknowingly negotiate each passage through Daath in the smaller Trees within Malkuth and the Personality/Astral Triad, over time we discover subtle changes in our day-to-day consciousness. Perhaps a new sense of inner peace, mental clarity or emotional balance emerges in daily life. We may feel more meaningfully grounded in our physical body (Malkuth) and the present moment as we move through the day.

Spontaneous attitudes of humility, gratitude, patience and wellbeing may wash over us or well up from within. We don't know where they come from but here they are, blessing us with gentle touches of our true self. We feel increasingly drawn and attracted to silent prayer, even if nothing much seems to happen there, or if our mind spews forth incessant streams of thoughts. It doesn't matter since everything passes and we vaguely sense the presence of something deeper going on inside us in this journey of faith and silent prayer, something apophatic that we can't quite grasp.

These are some signs of passages through Daath in the lights-off mode of contemplative prayer, and some signs of the prayer's fruits manifesting in daily life as inner obstacles are removed and grace flows more freely. It's all the work of the divine action in our soul. We simply need to trust and cooperate with the process as our consent to God's will in us grows deeper and stronger. Though the process may be hidden "in secret," its fruits are eventually revealed openly to us in our consciousness.

The lights-on mode of contemplative prayer is appreciably more dramatic and may be equally more distracting with intense emotions and flashy experiences of inspired exaltation or humiliating self-knowledge. The Wall of Energy and the images it spawns play significant roles in lights-on mysticism. Inner processes of death/change that are byproducts of passages through Daath, and that are undergone unconsciously in lights-off mysticism, are experienced consciously and sometimes overwhelmingly in lights-on prayer and daily life. The unloading of repressed memories, relationships, desires for compensation and so forth from the unconscious tends to be more dramatic and the purifications of the Dark Nights, as described by John of the Cross,[4] are liable to be experienced more vividly and intensely.

Chief among the inner purifications is the disruption and dismantling of the ego or false self's inner structures (habit patterns) of felt security, stability, self-confidence and orientation to reality. In each Sephira and smaller Tree of the personality construction, there's an inner foundation that grounds and limits consciousness to the particular reality orientation or perspective within that Sphere. Adaptation to the generic way of seeing things within a particular Sephira or combination of Sephiroth gives one a sense of security within that Sphere. Reality orientations within the Sephiroth may be, for example, in terms of the physical body, senses and outer world in Malkuth; in terms of the instincts of survival and reproduction in Yesod; focused on objective intellectual awareness, the ego and its need for power/control in Hod; or revolving around emotions, desires and the quest for affection/esteem/approval in Netzach. All of these things make the separate-self ego (false self) seem real and substantial.

When an individual's sense of ontological security is based on the stability of one's reality orientation within a particular Sephira or group of Sephiroth, the disruption and dismantling of these perceptual habit-patterns by the divine action may be perceived as threatening, horrific or even deadly from the vulnerable ego's standpoint. It may seem as if the fabric of reality is crumbling and one's sense of security and sanity are being lost along with it! This is where inner spiritual resources of trust in the divine action and grounding in the true integral center of one's being (Tiphareth) are crucial for weathering the storms of lights-on transitions through Daath, which is the inner birth canal of evolutionary change in the soul.

Habitual structures in the Walls of Thoughts and Energy are broken down by the divine action working through the profounder Wall of

Silence out of which energy and thoughts emerge, and which supports, contains and sustains the shifting Walls of Energy and Thoughts from within. This incredible process and the restructuring of consciousness it creates are the living mystery of Daath/the Cloud. As we literally do nothing in Daath but rest in empty silence in an attitude of humble receptivity and consent, much is being done in us by the Spirit—which is now free to access the foundational habit patterns in the unconscious recesses of Yesod in the Spheres of the Personality/Astral Triad in order to heal and transform them while flushing out or unloading their residue from the unconscious: When this toxic material passes out through consciousness and we let it go, it leaves us forever.

The Spirit's purification converts our unconscious intentions and motivation, the spirit in which we act, from attitudes of the false self to desires of the true self. Its healing repairs the damage of emotional trauma and wounding. The Spirit's work of transformation in us creates a new foundation for core personality patterns that will reflect the intentions and values of the divine image in our soul; and the unloading, as Thomas Keating says, evacuates the broken down psycho-spiritual debris of dismantled false-self personality patterns, happiness programs and their unruly afflictive emotions. This freeing death/rebirth process, which takes place in the Sephiroth of the Personality/Astral Triad and Malkuth while we rest consenting in Daath, is the actual process of our inner redemption and salvation.

The long term results of this contemplative process, which may be repeated several times on different levels of the soul in the Nights of Sense and Spirit, leads ultimately to the renewal of our personality and its rebirth in Christ (Tiphareth) at the center of the Tree in the Spiritual/Moral Triad. Each stage in this long journey is accompanied by some unloading of the unconscious as outmoded personality patterns are deconstructed and afflictive emotions from the past expelled. Our quiet resting in Daath, which is brought about by the divine action in us, and our consenting in humble sincerity and faith to whatever the Spirit does in us and our life, help greatly to facilitate this profound inner process of renewal and its continuing progress in our soul. The spiritual key to this wondrous work of death/change in us is our inner receptivity and consent to the divine action.

III

In strictly lights-off mysticism, the process of recurring passages through Daath and the accompanying inner purification, healing and transformation is undergone almost entirely unconsciously, until its fruits show up in daily consciousness. Before the fruits show up, one will typically experience surface symptoms of intermittent boredom, dryness, occasional emotional unloading via mild afflictive emotions, diminishment of self (ego or false self) and a non-descript hunger for silence, prayer and God in one's life. One may feel forlorn at times and be moved to say sadly to one's self, or a close friend, something like, "I miss God." This heartfelt spiritual hunger and inner vacancy is typical of "desert spirituality" and the Night of Sense, where God seems absent and the false self's old habits, pleasures and preoccupations cease to be fun or meaningful. In the Night of Sense, which is experienced primarily in Malkuth and the Personality/Astral Triad, we are like the ancient Israelites wandering lost in the desert, seeking the Promised Land of milk and honey, the spiritual ground of our soul.

While these unpleasantries are endured during critical passages of lights-off mysticism, the deeper work of constructive change in the soul proceeds secretly in the unconscious as we journey faithfully and unknowingly through Daath in daily prayer. It is, no doubt, a mercy, protection and grace that so many individuals on the contemplative journey experience their Dark Nights and passages through Daath primarily in the mode of lights-off mysticism, in spite of occasionally longing for a little more drama and excitement in their spiritual lives. This lights-off journey may spare them some unnecessary difficulties. In lights-off mysticism, conscious experiences of the Wall of Energy and its erratic fluctuations in one's body and consciousness are relatively minimal and mild, whereas in lights-on mysticism, they're relatively common and at times quite intense.

In lights-on mysticism, one is less protected from dramatic shifts in the Wall of Energy wrought by the divine action working change in the soul. Consequently, passages through Daath may at times be experienced as frightening immersions into a raging storm of chaotic energy and unloading with a tiny port of calm in its center. This is the same quiet center occupied by individuals in lights-off mysticism without feeling the disturbing storm. In either case, lights-on or lights-off, the inner work of purification, healing and transformation moves forward, so long as we consent and cooperate with the process in good faith.

As part of the divine action, Daath may create both storms (while we rest) and calm (where we rest) in the soul. This reveals its paradoxical dual nature: As an abyss of transformation, Daath secretly deconstructs and unloads outmoded thoughts and energy patterns into simple units of undifferentiated energy. As the dark invisible Sphere of apophatic contemplation, Daath *is* the Cloud of Unknowing where we rest effortlessly in deep silence and inner absorption. The ever-present subtle Wall of Silence is the natural portal of entry into and through Daath, and it is Daath itself. This Sphere of mystery holds profound peace beyond understanding and invisibly connects the soul to higher states of consciousness in the Supernal Triad. We do not and cannot force our way into Daath, but must wait for the divine action to draw us into the depths of its rest when the time is right. Rest leads inevitably to unloading until there's nothing left to unload.

Each outer and inner storm of upheaval, change and unloading that rocks the soul has a still point of calm in its center. One negotiates temporary emotional and mental storms of unloading in lights-on mysticism by simply accepting them as part of the process and resting, if one can, patiently in the peaceful center at the eye of the storm. This peaceful center is the opening to Christ within us. It corresponds to the heart chakra and is identified with Tiphareth in the smaller Tree of the Sphere one is climbing. This inner center, which lies beyond the unloading taking place in the personality Spheres, is our protection in Christ, the allegorical "rock" of 1 Corinthians 10:1-4, where it says, "Our ancestors were all under the cloud and all passed through the sea, and all were baptized into Moses in the cloud and in the sea, and all ate the same spiritual food and all drank the same spiritual drink. For they drank from the spiritual rock that followed them, and the rock was Christ."

Christ, the rock, is our inner fortress in the eye of all storms, especially those unleashed by the dismantling of the false self. This inner fortress is our true center of being in Tiphareth at the center of the Tree. As we rest in this center, trusting in the Lord, no storm of chaos and uncertainty can touch us. Tiphareth, the heart center, is our place of refuge during all passages through Daath/the Cloud where our familiar foundations and orientations to reality are lost and we enter unknowingly into a stream of uncertainty. Humility and faith form the shield of our fortress, the protection of the center covering our inner nakedness and exposed vulnerability.

Every crisis in our life is a storm through which we have to pass. This provides us opportunities for growth and may accompany passages through Daath. Outer life circumstances may trigger emotional and mental storms within us. These are generally temporary difficulties that come and go. The storms of unloading associated with our inner purification generally occur in ways that do not prevent our normal functioning in daily life. It may become temporarily more challenging and difficult to do what we do, but it's not prevented. The Spirit knows our limits and works with us accordingly.

Another metaphorical example for lights-on experiences, where individuals pass through difficult episodes of crisis and unloading with God's help, is the gospel account of Jesus walking on water and calming a stormy sea in Matthew 14:22–33. Focusing on the storm rather than on Jesus, Peter's faith falters; he sinks into the waves and, calling out for help, is pulled back up by Jesus. One lesson here is our need to keep faith and trust in God despite discouraging appearances in whatever outer or inner crises life brings us, knowing the Lord is always with us, offering divine help, support and opportunities for inner growth.

Often there will be alternations between lights-off and lights-on experiences in one's inner prayer life and outer life. It's normal for most people to be in the lights-off mode most of the time. In consenting to the divine presence and action, it's important to humbly trust that the Spirit always knows what's best and appropriate for our spiritual growth. It's only the childish false self in us that envies someone else's experiences or spiritual journey. Gratefully accepting responsibility for our self as God's gift to us frees us from neurotic self-judgments and helps speed us on our journey into the truth of the present moment, which is where we always are and where God always is.

As the divine universal consciousness, God is interested in experiencing human life with us, through us and in us, and in the unique ways that only each of us may provide. God already knows what it's like to be God. God also wants to know what it's like to be each of us. There's an incredible intimacy here in which God loves and treasures each of us just as we are and as we choose to become, whether we accept God's invitation and plan for spiritual growth or not. God—Father, Son and Holy Spirit—loves and is one with all of us, whoever we are.

Whatever we go through in life, God goes through it too because God is living our life with us, secretly in a mysterious way that's hidden from our sight. This is how God knows us through and through, each and all of us all at the same time in each moment of our lives. God is us and we, on the deepest level, are God, too. Everything is lights-on for God because God is Limitless Light bound by no barriers.

IV

Though known under different names, there's an element of Daath / the Cloud running through the contemplative dimension of at least some, and probably all, of the world's major religious and spiritual traditions. That is, there are non-conceptual notions and practices, equivalent to Christian apophatic contemplation and Daath in Qabalah, to be found in other traditions. For example, Theravada Buddhism has a non-conceptual practice called "bare attention," which follows after the concentrative disciplines of reflecting on the Buddha's teachings and practicing various forms of mindfulness meditation (such as focusing on one's breathing in and out, eating, walking and other activities). This "bare attention" meditative practice is intended to liberate the mind from existential ignorance by penetrating the Walls of Thoughts and Energy in the present moment to reveal the truth of one's ever-present, underlying, non-created Buddha Nature. In Mahayana Buddhism, there's the notion of *shunyata* or emptiness which, like Daath / the Cloud, reveals the inner emptiness of all created phenomena. In the *Perfection of Wisdom* text (*Prajnaparamita Sutra*), a principle Mahayana scripture, we're told that "form is emptiness and emptiness is form," a profound teaching about non-ego and the deeper nature of created reality. Prajnaparamita is called "the Mother of the Buddhas,"[5] meaning that the conscious realization of this profound plenum void or emptiness is the inner foundation of every Buddha's Enlightenment.

In Taoism, there's the central Feminine Principle of Receptivity or *wu wei*, also referred to as "inaction," which reflects the basic disposition of contemplative prayer or "resting in God." There's also the apophatic notion of "the Tao that cannot be named," which is the hidden Source of the nameable Tao, i.e., Nature, her laws and the perceptible Universe.[6] It's taught by China's ancient sages that the way to unite with the Tao—equivalent to becoming one with God in the West—is by imitating the Tao; that is, by circulating the inner light of heaven in the soul's energy body (a kataphatic yoga practice) and by practicing "inaction"—the humble receptivity of non-conceptual, silent meditation[7]—equivalent to apophatic prayer or contemplation in Christian Mysticism.

In Himalayan yoga and Hindu mysticism, where "all methods end in silence," *Sahaja Samadhi* is a permanent stage of enlightenment experienced while one is active in the human body. *Sahaja* is a natural condition of ongoing spontaneous awareness that rests continually in the open space of universal awareness or emptiness (before thoughts arise) while living daily life. *Sahaja Samadhi* is a basis of *Advaita Vedanta* in Hinduism, the profound philosophy and meditative practice of non-dualism that realizes the one ultimate Godhead of *Sat-Chit-Ananda* (absolute knowledge, absolute consciousness and absolute bliss) while transcending all attachments to ego (the false self) and the factual illusions of created reality.[8]

I once heard a highly accomplished yoga meditation master from India, Swami Amar Jyoti, who meditated in Himalayan caves for about twelve years as a young man, describe the inner passage into the highest states of consciousness. He said it was like going through a "Z-shaped" vacuum cave in the brain between the third-eye and the crown chakra. He said it was a dark, difficult movement into uncertainty where you don't know where you're going and all you're familiar and comfortable with, i.e., your sense of security as a separate-self identity, falls away. The Swami said the ego dissolves (if it surrenders) or is overwhelmed (if it tries to struggle) in this dark tunnel of the inner abyss, which he compared to the crisis of passing through a "bottleneck."[9] As a result of passing through this vacuum cave in the brain, he said that the inner secret of creation is revealed and all phenomena are seen as being luminously transparent, profoundly interrelated and existing in God.

The above account by Swami Amar Jyoti sounds like an excellent description of a lights-on/lights-off passage through Daath/the Cloud on the Tree of Life. The emptiness realization of *shunyata* in Mahayana Buddhism, the "Z-shaped" vacuum cave in the brain of advanced yoga meditation, and the passage through Daath/the Cloud in Jewish Mysticism and Christian contemplation, all ultimately put an end to the illusion of absolute ego-identity or false self; and all of these inner paths to spiritual awakening bring the individual soul into a new, more highly integrated and evolved stage of being and consciousness which, in Centering Prayer, we call the true self, divine indwelling or transformation (rebirth) in Christ.

We can't say what Daath actually is because it's the enigmatic dark Sephira symbolized by a dense, foggy Cloud and associated with crossing the abyss separating one level of created reality from another on the Tree of Life. We may say that Daath correlates to apophatic contemplation, a state of receptive unknowing, rest and consent to God's will in us that frees the divine action to purify, heal and transform us. How this all happens is ultimately a mystery but why it happens is simply because it is God's will and plan for us to enter the Promised Land of our divine inheritance—provided we freely accept the divine invitation and cooperate with its implementation by doing our part.

Though we cannot actually know what Daath/the Cloud is, we may know something about what Daath does. Daath does by nondoing; this is part of its unknowable mystery and paradoxical reality. In Malkuth, Daath correlates to the Zero Point Field in quantum mechanics—the infinitely small empty point of being and source of becoming that is omnipresent throughout the physical Universe as a dimension of consciousness. It is pure paradox. In Yesod, Daath correlates to the individual and collective unconscious of life forms on Earth and throughout the Universe. In Hod, it's the space between thoughts; and in Netzach, Daath correlates to the hole in the soul, the hole of inner separation and incompleteness that gives rise to the longing of desire in each soul.

There are at least ten degrees or grades of Daath corresponding to Daath in the small Trees in the ten Sephiroth; and there is what we may call "big Daath" as the Great Abyss separating the Spiritual/Moral and Supernal Triads of the microcosmic individual soul and the great Universal Tree or Macrocosm. Each degree or grade of Daath corresponds to a deepening, more comprehensive level of apophatic contemplation—which moves through the invisible darkness of created reality into the incomprehensible Limitless Light and perfection of non-created Reality; from total emptiness into fullness of love, truth and freedom, and from nothingness into everything. In Daath itself, God's light shining bright is darkness to the soul.

The Cloud, as symbol of God's apophatic presence, appears again in Acts 1:9-10 at the time of Jesus' ascension: "He was lifted up as they looked on, and a cloud took him from their sight. They were...staring into the sky as he went." This is not merely a physical ascension into the sky of Malkuth but a spiritual ascension above the Spiritual/Moral Triad into the universal consciousness of the Supernal Triad and Limitless Light where "the fullness of (Christ)...fills all things in every way" (Eph. 1:23).

12

REBIRTH IN CHRIST

I

Just as there's an element of Daath/the Cloud in each of the ten visible Sephiroth on the Tree of Life, so is there an element of Tiphareth/Beauty. Tiphareth is the alchemical Sphere in the Tree's center that combines and integrates the soul's energies and re-creates its personality expression and consciousness as it evolves up the Tree. As Tiphareth evolves in the smaller Trees of the ascending Sephiroth in the Personality/Astral and Spiritual/Moral Triads, one's personality and consciousness also evolve. Each step in this journey involves a re-creation of the personality expression on a higher level of integration and wholeness. The soul's movement up the Tree through Tiphareth in the ascending Spheres is the process of its continuing inner resurrection and rebirth in Christ. This inner evolutionary process ultimately leads to the soul's ascension into the universal-consciousness Spheres of the Supernal Triad.

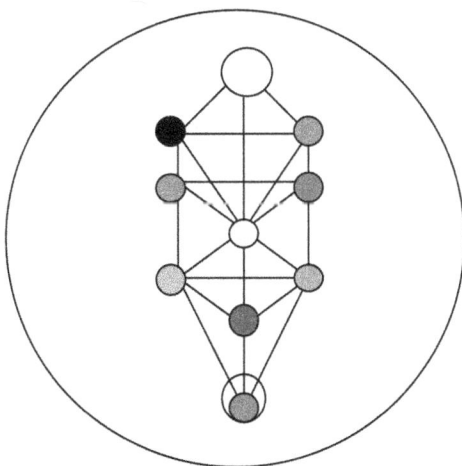

Smaller Tree Within a Sephira

As explained in chapter 4, *Tiphareth* in Hebrew is *Ben,* the Son of *Ab,* Divine Father (Chokmah), and *Ama,* Divine Mother (Binah). *Tiphareth* also means "Messiah," "Redeemer," "Prince of Peace," "Anointed One," the "Sun" and "Word of the Father" through whom created reality and individual souls come into being and evolve in the Worlds of Formation and Manifestation. The Greek word for *Tiphareth,* the anointed one, is *Christos,* which is Latin for "Christ." So our rebirth in and through Tiphareth is our rebirth in Christ, who became human flesh in the historical Jesus of Nazareth.

The individual soul returns to its roots and realizes the potential of its divine inheritance through its rebirth in Christ on the Tree of Life. Christ, or Tiphareth, is the true center of the Tree in both Macrocosm and microcosm. The soul evolves to its Tiphareth through the refinement of its personality expression in the Personality / Astral Triad and beyond. According to Qabalistic teaching, this generally requires multiple re-creations of the personality expression, perhaps in this life and the next, until the true self is fully realized in consciousness. The true self is our rebirth in Christ, the awakening of the divine image dwelling in the soul where the personality expression becomes a unique expression of Christ in us and our life in Christ—what Paul in Colossians 1:27 refers to as "Christ in us, our hope of glory."

Our rebirth in Christ is a function of the gift of contemplation, the gift of the Spirit's presence and action in our soul. Our personality expression is re-created each time meaningful change and growth occur in the patterns that govern it. This has to take place first in Malkuth and the Personality / Astral Triad, in the Night of Sense. Then it continues in the Night of Spirit, which takes place in the Spiritual / Moral Triad. The Night of Spirit is said to eliminate the last subtle vestiges of the false self.[1] However, as long as we're human, as long as we have any will separate from God's will, we remain capable of falling into error and sin, capable of every evil to which the ego may be tempted and succumb. It's important to remember this and to take refuge in deep humility, which is our surest safeguard against vanities of self-deception and temptations to evil.[2]

11

Our rebirth in Christ begins in Malkuth, when consciousness enters Tiphareth in the smaller Tree within that Sphere, and we begin experiencing the first stirrings of love and existential meaning in our heart center. These first conscious contacts with Tiphareth in Malkuth are our initial spiritual awakenings in human ground. They take us, if only briefly, beyond our separate-self sense, allowing us to appreciate and care for others, for the goodness of life in our physical body and the world around us. We experience touches of the preciousness of God's creation through Nature, physical pleasures and the enjoyment of those who are close to us. The strength of our inner connection to Tiphareth grows with repeated contacts, bringing new wellbeing, value and happiness into consciousness.

As human awareness experiences more contacts with the Tiphareth in Malkuth's smaller Tree, the individual's consciousness begins opening to its spiritual level, sensing the presence of a deeper, more enduring reality within, behind and beyond the changing seasons of physical reality. Feelings of oneself as a spiritual being belonging in the physical world begin emerging into consciousness. One may experience various forms of mystical communion with Nature and the environment, discovering a spontaneous empathy for other life forms and one's fellow human beings.

With further development, the aspect of Christ as "Prince of Peace" awakens in the Tiphareth of Malkuth. Individuals deeply touched by Tiphareth in Malkuth extend their love and compassion beyond the circles of their immediate family and friends, their home society and group affiliations, out to humanity in general. These individuals are inspired to work for the betterment of humanity in all areas. They tend to experience humanity as one family of diverse peoples within the unity of our spiritual solidarity in Christ. This deep global identification inspires them to dedicate themselves to world peace, justice and the wellbeing of all peoples on Earth, and to our common home, the Earth itself.

Feelings of goodwill, love and compassion for others move us to desire and work for peace and justice in practical ways; for example, by promoting cooperation and mutual understanding among people of differing backgrounds, e.g., cultural, social, religious or racial. The driving influence of Geburah flowing into Tiphareth in the small Tree of Malkuth motivates one to seek justice and righteousness in the world. At the same time, Chesed inspires a spiritual idealism of altruistic love in the individual that may seem naive and unrealistic, if not foolish, to others who have not yet awakened to a fuller consciousness of Tiphareth within them on this level.

All authentic love in human relationships comes initially from Tiphareth (Christ) in the small Tree of Malkuth. There are, of course, degrees to this love as it evolves from self-centered desire into mutual caring and ultimately into the self-transcending love of higher spiritual ideals. Each step in the development of our love nature is a step forward in our awakening to Tiphareth and rebirth in Christ. The growth of love in us is the growth of our life in Christ, which continues on and on as we evolve up the Tree of our soul's energy field.

On the personal level, awakening to Tiphareth in the Tree of Malkuth gives one a new feeling of inner wholeness, self-understanding and completion. The vantage point of consciousness in Tiphareth allows us to view the personality construction below in the Personality/Astral Triad of the smaller Tree from the overall perspective of this higher Sphere (Tiphareth). This creates a new view and point of balance for consciousness in the personality, so that one is not so easily caught up and over-identified with shifting thoughts and emotions triggered by the false self's happiness programs and reactions to outer events. Hence, in the Tiphareth of Malkuth, one gains new objectivity and inner freedom in relation to the personality as well as the beginnings of spiritual rebirth in Christ.

Functioning out of Tiphareth in Malkuth involves an inner movement away from childish or adolescent false-self orientations into a level of adult maturity where satisfaction, self-esteem and happiness come from caring and doing things to benefit others. In other words, to really grow-up as a human is to evolve into the benevolent maturity of Tiphareth in human ground by outgrowing the shallow desires and agendas of the false self and replacing them with the inner wholeness of a spiritual integration that is complete in itself and finds outer fulfillment through the love and service of others. Such a person is a truly free human being.

Individuals who attain to Tipharerth in Malkuth benefit humanity by both their outer actions and their inner spiritual practices. The energy of peace and love radiating through them serves human evolution by inspiring and uplifting others around them and the collective soul of humanity as well. They help to bring Christ into the world.

III

The sense of life's passion and preciousness grows as consciousness touches base with Tiphareth in the smaller Tree of Yesod. Here, in the Tiphareth of Yesod, the unconscious instinctual energies of our animal nature are gradually ordered and integrated into mutual harmony so that violent passions of the survival instinct and sex/desire are subdued and tamed by the calming presence of Tiphareth's influence. We become free to enjoy the legitimate sensations/pleasures of our animal nature without being dominated by unruly passions and afflictive emotions rooted in the primal survival instinct and its drives for food, sex and power, cruelty and kindness. The pre-programming of our instinctual needs and animal nature form the basis of the personality patterns and tendencies that are held in Yesod.

Tipharerth in Yesod is instrumental in restructuring unconscious personality patterns by eliminating the unhealthy ones and replacing them with patterns that are in harmony with the true self or divine image. Patterns that hinder spiritual progress are dissolved by the divine action working through Tiphareth in the smaller Tree of Yesod. Tiphareth is a benevolent guiding light in the darkness of Yesod, where blind instincts and unruly passions of the animal soul drive unconscious patterns of automatic reaction to the false self's happiness programs of unfulfilled desires. The penetrating light of Tiphareth's integrative energy working in Yesod is able to get inside the astral-matter structures of these patterns and change them, as described in earlier chapters. Consenting to the presence and action of Christ in our soul, as is done in Centering Prayer, greatly facilitates this process.

Yesod is the dark valley of the unconscious, the Underworld of legend, and the treacherous jungle of wild instinctual energies and passions in the individual and collective human soul. Out of it arise the blind and sometimes violent compensatory drives of the false self's childish happiness programs. The most primitive instincts of survival and reproduction, of cruelty and kindness, reside in the animal-soul matrix of Yesod, which holds the evolutionary history of all life on Earth. Tiphareth in the Tree of Yesod expresses as Christ the Redeemer who orders, tames and transforms these wild energies and drives with the healing touch of benevolence and love, calming stormy passions and comforting restless souls living in fear of pain and death. "Peace, be still," and the storm suddenly ceases (Luke 8:24–25). This is the work of Tiphareth in the Tree of Yesod.

When the inner waters are still, when there's absolute calm in the animal soul of Yesod, then we may enter deep into the Wall of Silence and Daath in contemplation as Tiphareth accesses the foundational patterns in the soul's personality construction. Then healing may occur and the divine image may be imprinted in place of outmoded patterns created in fear, anger and desperation to compensate for wounded unmet needs. This movement of the divine action of Tiphareth in Yesod goes to the foundation of the false self itself, gradually peeling away each sticky layer of the candy-coated evil onion that burns our eyes with frustrations and disappointments of happiness programs that can't possibly work because they fail to address our soul's true needs.

The transformation of unconscious personality patterns in Yesod is the nub of our rebirth in Christ because these patterns extend to the Yesods in the smaller Trees of all the personality Sephiroth and beyond. The restructuring of these patterns in Yesod by Tiphareth is what creates lasting change in the soul's personality construction and consciousness. The establishment of healthy new patterns in Yesod creates a chain reaction that reverberates from the unconscious up into consciousness, freeing one from the false self's mistaken beliefs, attitudes, happiness programs and afflictive emotions. Hence, the work of Tiphareth in Yesod is the process of our inner redemption, the foundation and backbone of our rebirth in Christ and evolution up the Tree of Life.

IV

In Hod/Splendor, Tiphareth manifests as Christ the Sun of Truth, the inner light of intelligence illuminating creation and our understanding. Our mind becomes clear, ordered and in sync with the wisdom and values of conscience under the influence of Tiphareth in the smaller Tree of Hod. Tiphareth in Hod rejuvenates the intellect, opening it to new possibilities by lifting it out of habitual ruts of thought and belief that restrict the scope of its creative and conceptual capacities.

In Hod, Tiphareth works to free the intellect from culturally conditioned superstitions, prejudices and beliefs that limit the mind, closing it off from openness to new ideas and insights that may broaden its perspective and enlighten its understanding. In order to accomplish this, Tiphareth needs to penetrate the Sphere of Yesod in Hod's smaller Tree where the intellect's unconscious programming and patterns reside. This can be challenging because it requires the individual to willingly let-go and outgrow culturally conditioned patterns of thought and belief he or she shares with others as part of their collective identity (sense of intimacy/belonging) in society. It requires learning to think independently for oneself by refining the intellect's creative thought processes and outgrowing the flawed aspects of society's group-mind and cultural conditioning.

Our mind's habitual preconceptions in Hod create a consciousness-filter through which we perceive and interpret reality. These culturally conditioned and self-created preconceptions give us a sense of knowing what's going on, a sense of what's real and what's not; but they also trap consciousness in ruts of repetition that prevent it from awakening to new insights or "thinking outside the box" of society's consensus reality model. Since the ego often finds its sense of security in conforming to the group-mind's consensus model, to venture beyond it intellectually often requires a leap of faith and independence of thought. This tests our soul's inner mettle and intellectual integrity, since spiritual growth and consciousness evolution in Hod need openness to new discoveries beyond limiting filters of the group-mind, unfounded preconceptions and the false self's ego-security, regardless of how sacred or indispensible we may regard these things.

In its purity, intellectual integrity requires an unconditional commitment to Truth in itself over undue attachment to its humanly created representations. Intellectual integrity in the Sphere of Hod figures prominently in the development of scientific thought, discovery and dedication to finding the truth, whatever it may be. Such intellectual integrity in the quest for Truth is a primary spiritual value requiring humble discipline and commitment to pursuing and uncovering the truth of reality on all levels. When preconceptions of any type stand in the way of this quest, they must be given up or at least temporarily suspended, if any real progress is to be made. New learning and growth are supported by the discipline of an unprejudiced mind honestly admitting to the uncertainty of unknowing. This calls for willingness to examine all assumptions and preconceptions, wherever they come from, with meticulous care, exploring and evaluating their implications as if creating a map of uncharted territory.

In their defense, culturally conditioned preconceptions and other ideas do serve a legitimate and necessary function in the budding progress of our intellectual and spiritual development; but their proper role is as stepping stones for temporary support as we proceed through and beyond them, not as stopping stones where we get stuck and remain unduly attached beyond the point of their practical usefulness. For optimal inner growth, we need to be ready and willing to suspend our assumptions and let all preconceived ideas and cherished convictions go, if and when the Spirit calls us to do so. This may require courage and a leap of faith. Remaining stuck in limiting preconceptions easily degenerates into a kind of idolatry of ideas that eventually calcify into rigid dogmas, prejudices and superstitions. The inevitable result of this will be stagnation and retardation of our intellectual and spiritual growth in the mental Sphere of Hod. One encouraging thing we may safely say regarding ideas, opinions and preconceptions we're reluctant to release is that God is full of surprises, wonderful surprises that await us. This possibility challenges our faith and trust in God.

Limiting patterns of preconception, reasoning and belief that are based on false assumptions are broken down and discarded by the action of Tiphareth in Yesod in the Tree of Hod. Some examples of these are prejudices and superstitions, assumptions and conclusions based on values of the false self, its agendas for happiness, and thinking that trusts only the dualistic perspectives of materialism and physical reality. Tiphareth elevates our intellectual processes in Hod out of such ruts so they may function freely, independently and more in harmony with Cosmic Spiritual Law. The inspiration of Tiphareth helps one to understand intuitively that we are not isolated individuals but connected telepathically and spiritually to one another. This promotes goodwill and desires for peace and cooperation, along with openness to new ideas and ways of thinking.

The comprehensive awareness of reality flowing from Tiphareth gives the intellect an overview of whatever it contemplates. Energy and awareness received through Tiphareth in Hod heal divisions in the intellect and help it to mature into a useful and effective instrument of conscious intelligence. Guidance from Tiphareth helps the intellect to be used constructively as an aid to spiritual growth, giving one an objective view of life's larger reality and choices. The intellectual learning and growth process inspired by Tiphareth in Hod contributes significantly to the healthy fulfillment of one's basic instinctual need for power/control. It does this by giving the individual conscious freedom and independence in using the intellect to evaluate and judge priorities, choices, beliefs and one's course of action in life.

As this process progresses, an inner balancing takes place in the mind, allowing us to intuitively grasp important spiritual truths such as the fact that we are not our intellect, our ideas of God are not God, and the ego of our human personality is not our true identity, as previously assumed, but a necessary self-created instrument we need for functioning in the world. Tiphareth helps the intellect to plant images and thought forms in the unconscious that will aid in personal and spiritual development. Tiphareth in Hod, functioning as Christ the Sun, illuminates new mysteries to the intellect, opening its intuitive consciousness to higher ideas and inspirations from the Spiritual/Moral Triad. Through Tiphareth in Hod, the mind may enter invisible Spheres of the Spiritual/Moral Triad, receiving insights and guidance from these realms that are of practical use in the individual's immediate human life.

In receptive prayer and meditation in the Sphere of Hod, our focus slips beneath the Walls of Thought and Energy, entering the deep space between thoughts (the Wall of Silence and Daath/the Cloud). This apophatic immersion in our spiritual depths frees us from preoccupations with the ego and its games. With no need to cling to the ego or false self and its enveloping Wall of Thoughts, we may relax and simply rest detached in the presence of what is, quietly observing our mind until sinking deeper into silence. Absorbed in apophatic silence, the mind is refreshed with deep inner peace and sacred energy, providing a fresh view of self and reality. After gaining a new perspective from inner renewal and the detachment of objective self-observation, Tiphareth in the smaller Tree of Hod allows us to see and understand with ironic humor our former follies and needless ego-clinging to false-self desires and illusions in the Personality/Astral Triad.

As the mind becomes more ordered and we move further in the direction of spiritual growth, Tiphareth in Hod begins to educate and enrich the human intellect with the beginning seeds of the Mind of Christ, the inner light of Christ the Sun. According to Thomas Keating, the Mind of Christ is associated with the Seven Gifts of the Spirit: reverence, fortitude, piety, counsel, knowledge, understanding and wisdom.[3] These gifts or aspects of the Mind of Christ belong to the higher stages of spiritual development in the Spiritual/Moral Triad and beyond. Yet they may begin to manifest and shine as consciousness enters Tiphareth in the Sphere of Hod/Splendor.

The last three of the Spirit's gifts, Knowledge, Understanding and Wisdom, far transcend the intellect and are known as the contemplative gifts of the Spirit. They mature on the Tree of Life as follows: Knowledge is realized in Daath/the Cloud as a deep intuitive knowing that comes from unknowing; Understanding is perfected in Binah/Understanding; and Wisdom matures in Chokmah/Wisdom. These gifts, which far transcend Hod and the Personality/Astral Triad, belong to the precious treasure of our spiritual inheritance in Christ, the Sun of Truth.

V

Entering Tiphareth in the Tree of Netzach/Victory opens the way for emotional healing and purification of our desire nature. As we become increasingly less identified with our false self and its ego-centric demands (happiness programs), these lower values and goals are gradually replaced by higher ideals of love, conscience and the true self. We begin to long increasingly for spiritual growth and are inspired within by altruistic love, goodness and compassion for others. The inner vision of our true self and life in Christ begins dawning in consciousness as new energies and life are breathed into us by the divine indwelling awakening in our soul. We may sense these movements consciously or unconsciously.

A fundamental shift in our inner motivation, values and sense of identity begins to take place spontaneously in Netzach as our being is charged from within by the influx of higher spiritual vibrations, re-creating the foundation and structure of our personality patterns. This may occur in either a lights-on or lights-off mode as we humbly pray, meditate and live our life consciously in relation to God's presence within and around us. The fruits of this change are gently felt in consciousness as we sense increasingly that everything is a gift and grace of the Spirit working in and around us. We become the way of Christ by following the way in contemplation and action, knowing we're always in God's presence whether we feel it or not.

Netzach is the Sphere of our emotions, will, imagination and desire nature. In the small Tree of Netzach, opposite Hod, Tiphareth manifests as Christ the Messiah, the Anointed One of God whose mission is to free the soul and bring it to salvation in the Spiritual/Moral Triad—salvation being freedom from false-self patterns plus entering an abiding consciousness of our life in Christ. Our human will grows into harmony with conscience and God's will through the influence of Tiphareth in Netzach integrating the personality into our true self.

As this happens, the nine Fruits of the Spirit begin manifesting in consciousness. These Fruits are: love, joy, peace, patience, kindness, goodness, faithfulness, humility and self-control (Gal. 5:22–23). Like the Gifts of the Spirit mentioned above, these Fruits mature in the Spiritual/Moral Triad and beyond through the full ripening richness of our life in Christ in the center of the Tree. However, their buds may begin flowering through the inner work of Tiphareth in Netzach's Tree at the top of the Personality/Astral Triad. Netzach is the Sphere where consciousness is prepared for permanent transition into the Spiritual/Moral Triad.

Yesod in Netzach's Tree is the stronghold of the false self's emotional programs for happiness. The powerful emotions that motivate the false self's unconscious will and desires reside in Yesod in the Tree of Netzach as coiled energy patterns encoded with images derived from the individual's unmet and wounded needs for security/survival, pleasure, affection/esteem, power/control and intimacy/belonging. The intuitive symbolic language of these images determines what represents one's happiness programs and their gratification to the false self in one's outer life in Malkuth. The compacted energy fed into and built-up within the false self's images of desire is what empowers them and determines the strength of their intensity and influence in the soul. This includes the afflictive emotions attached to them.

When we stop feeding fresh energy into the false self's happiness programs, they begin expending the energy built-up within them and gradually weaken out as their energy decreases. Hence, the work of Tiphareth in the Tree of Netzach, which requires our conscious cooperation, begins by depriving the false self's images of fresh energy through cutting off their food supply; that is, by diverting the energy of conscious attention, will, choices and behavior away from their agendas. This requires conscious desire and effort by the personality, including a willingness to endure pangs of withdrawal from addictions to false-self habit patterns. Going through this process of self-denial regarding habitual desires of the false self helps us to develop inner freedom and self-control.

The next phase of Tiphareth's work in Netzach involves deconstructing the symbolic images of the false self's happiness programs via vibratory shattering of the images' astral-matter structures in the unconscious, as explained in earlier chapters. As the demolition of the false self's personality patterns in Netzach's Yesod progresses,

Tiphareth in the small Tree of Netzach begins constructing new images of the true self in their place. These new images are powered with the motivating energy of the soul's attraction and desire for spiritual growth and higher ideals of love, unity and justice. In this way, immature self-centered desires in the Personality/Astral Triad are replaced with higher values and ideals of the Spiritual/Moral Triad in Netzach/Victory. This is a true spiritual victory that heals wounded emotions and purifies one's desire nature.

The successive replacement of happiness-program patterns with higher ideals and desires of the true self gradually creates a chain reaction in the unconscious recesses of Yesod in Netzach that reverberates up into consciousness, changing one's conscious motivation and desires from within. This change is quite spontaneous and automatic, happening suddenly and unexpectedly, like the answer to a prayer. One no longer feels bound or attracted to the same things as before; there's peace inside, patience, and a new sense of freedom and wellbeing. A palpable rebirth is taking place in one's personality and desire nature, seemingly out of nowhere. It's the work of Tiphareth in the Tree of our emotional desire nature, the Tree of Netzach. This inner rebirth frees us from domination by the false self and its afflictive emotions, empowering us to finally "walk the talk" of our better intentions and higher ideals. It's a true spiritual victory of our rebirth in Christ.

VI

Guidance and support from Tiphareth in Netzach helps one to remain emotionally balanced. It also supports how emotions interact with thoughts and influence Hod (the intellect) in the personality.[4] In Netzach, emotions guided by Tiphareth enter the unconscious and help to change negative emotional response patterns into constructive patterns. This emotional renewal is instrumental in disempowering and dismantling the false self's happiness programs and preventing their afflictive emotions from triggering destructive emotional responses in one's daily life and relationships.

Freed from the burdens and distractions of destructive afflictive emotions, the person is able to more easily focus on spiritual ideals and goals. He or she feels emotionally attracted to Tiphareth (Christ) in the Spiritual/Moral Triad. In turn, Tiphareth, the heart center, acts as a source of inspiration to emotionally support and sustain the individual, especially in periods of difficulty like the Dark Nights of Sense and Spirit. This provides emotional strength to the Gift of Fortitude in holding up under discouraging circumstances and striving for the difficult good.

Tiphareth in Netzach may infuse heightened levels of lights-on spiritual idealism (from Chesed) into the individual's consciousness. Such experiences, when needed, serve to keep one motivated in the spiritual journey to not give up when frustrations arise and efforts seem fruitless. We are mysteriously drawn by the love of Christ to seek our true center in him; that is, in Tiphareth in the Spiritual/Moral Triad within us. Eventually, as we continue in regular daily practice of contemplative prayer while focusing our life on spiritual ideals and goals, we experience an emotional rebirth into a fuller awareness of the heart center and Christ's presence in us. Our sense of identity gradually shifts to the true self and heart center (Tiphareth), and we feel more spiritually connected on a conscious level.

Inner connection to Tiphareth in Netzach causes us to feel emotionally connected to others spiritually as Tiphareth opens the way for the growth of empathy and compassion in our soul. "Compassion" means "to feel with," to share in the passions of another or others. This comes as a natural result of our inner identity with others in the Mystical Body of Christ where we are not really separate from anyone else. Christ lives in all of us and makes us one. Our inner unity in Christ is clearly expressed by Jesus in Matthew 25:40, where he says, "Truly I tell you, just as you did it to one of the least of these, who are members of my family, you did it to me."

What we call "love" is the highest and most sublime human emotion. We may wonder: where do our emotions come from? They have both heavenly and earthly origins. In terms of terrestrial evolution on the Tree of Life, our emotions have come from the instinctual passions and automatic response drives of the animal soul in Yesod. These primitive passions are refined and articulated into a complex array of diverse emotions on the human level by Hod and Netzach.

There's a progressive movement of charged life-force energy, beginning with the wild primal passions in Yesod (the survival/reproductive instinct), moving up into Hod (the intellect) and flowing into Netzach where the energy is articulated into particular emotions. There are also energy paths connecting Yesod to Netzach and Yesod to Hod where energies may flow back and forth as these three Spheres influence one another. Thus, our human emotions begin as generic animal passions in Yesod and are subsequently refined by Hod and Netzach into specific emotions in the Tree of Netzach.

We also have ennobling spiritual emotions that come down into Netzach from the Spiritual/Moral Triad as we're ready and able to receive them. Emotions, which can devolve into irrational passions or evolve into higher spiritual ideals, are the energy of desire that drives, inspires and moves us to action. Hence, they are fundamental and indispensible. Tiphareth (Christ) in Netzach is the guiding intelligence within us that orders, refines, balances and directs our emotions in accord with God's plan for our spiritual growth.

As our emotions are refined spiritually by Tiphareth in Netzach, we experience them within the context of our connection to spiritual ground and their effects in us are tempered by an orientation to reality that's centered in an awareness of God's presence. This dramatically changes both how we interpret our emotions and how we respond to them. We discover that Tiphareth, the heart center, is actively working through our emotions, keeping us centered within so that, while feeling emotionally connected to others, we're able to avoid being swayed by negative afflictive emotions occurring in the group-mind.

Through Tiphareth in Netzach, the idealism of spiritual love rejuvenates our desire nature, lifting it toward the divine indwelling in the Spiritual/Moral Triad. As we experience the inspiration of Christ working through our emotions, we're able to transmit their positive energy to others around us and into the group-mind, to help transmute negative emotions. We may do this openly or secretly, depending on circumstances and our role in life.

Our discussion of Tiphareth in Netzach/Victory would be incomplete without mentioning the greatest spiritual victory in human history, that of Jesus Christ, the Anointed One and Messiah

in this world and the next: The spiritual victory of Christ in Netzach is the victory of divine love over sin and death. It's the victory of Jesus on the Cross, conquering evil through the sacrifice
of ego. "Father, forgive them, they know not what they do" (Luke
23:34). The continuing victory of Jesus in the Supernal Triad of
the small Tree in Netzach is the victory of his resurrection from
death and ascension into heaven in the Spiritual/Moral Triad and
beyond where his glorified humanity has become the universal consciousness of Christ the King in the heart of all souls. The individual human soul of Jesus of Nazareth has become the divine soul
and Mystical Body of Christ in Tiphareth on the Universal Tree of
Life. The spiritual fruit of this victory is open to all through Christ
within us, in the true center of our soul.

VII

The transition from Netzach/Victory at the top of the Personal-
ity/Astral Triad into Tiphareth/Beauty in the Spiritual/Moral Triad
is a major step in our spiritual journey of rebirth in Christ. It's the
transition from our human nature and inheritance into our divine
nature and inheritance, shifting our center of identity from the ego
or false self into our new and true self. This rebirth is the work of the
divine action in us. Once the necessary preparation has been completed in the Personality/Astral Triad, our transition into Tiphareth
in the Spiritual/Moral Triad is the next step in our soul's journey of
return up the Tree of Life. We're still fully human while living in this
world, but in a new way with a new focus.

Entering Tiphareth in the Spiritual/Moral Triad is our soul's great
homecoming to its true center in Christ, where we take our place as
a citizen of the New Jerusalem or heavenly kingdom; that is, as a
conscious member of the Mystical Body of Christ and the Communion of Saints fulfilled in the luminous warmth of God's love. Lights-
on intuitions of immortality impregnate the soul with the energy of
Christ's resurrection and glory in the New Jerusalem. This joyous
state of consciousness, "impregnated with divine love," frees the
soul of all worry, utterly transcending the isolation of separate-self

ego-consciousness that kept it divided in human ground and the Personality/Astral Triad.

In the lights-on mode of contemplative prayer, entering the Tree of Tiphareth in the Spiritual/Moral Triad is a blissful sharing, if only briefly, in divine corporate consciousness with countless souls in the heavenly Jerusalem where Christ is King. In the timeless glory of Christ's love shines the inner fountain of infinite happiness, rejoicing in the astounding discovery that no matter what happens in the tragic-comic dramas of human life on Earth, everything is ultimately all right and could never be otherwise, since love is truth in God forever beyond the passing show of created appearances. This love, which transcends duality and human reason, is ultimately where we come from, who we are and where we belong.

In love's blessed land of heart's treasure, there's nothing to desire for one's self alone because here we are rich beyond telling, happy beyond dreaming in the awakening light of divine life and love overflowing the soul. There's nothing left to desire for oneself because one is utterly whole and complete, enjoying the gifts of divine inheritance unfolding in the heavenly kingdom (Malkuth) in the smaller Tree within Tiphareth. The one good thing we may desire in this state is for all souls who do not yet know its happiness, all those whose life and consciousness are confined to the lonely struggles and pain of the lower Malkuth and Personality/Astral Triad, may come to share in this banquet of unspeakable blessing in the glorious love, truth and freedom of Christ's living presence. With repeated contacts in prayer, meditation or daily life, our spiritual connection to Tiphareth and the heart chakra is gradually strengthened, eventually developing into a more or less permanent link.

In this heavenly lights-on state, we learn that to love God is to love what God loves and to want what God wants; and what God wants is for God's creation to be perfected by the fulfillment of God's plan in all that's created. As goodness overflows and gives of itself, God longs for everyone to know we're all in God and God's in all of us, loving us, giving us freedom to create our destiny—to say "Yes" or "No" to life, to accept or reject the invitation and gift of divine inheritance.

The tragedy in this drama is that so many souls on Earth do not yet know or believe in the truth of God's loving invitation and their own divine inheritance. Our spiritual inheritance is a full share, according to our capacity, in the exhaustless riches of the Lord's kingdom, power and glory as revealed in spiritual ground; that is, as revealed in the Spiritual/Moral and Supernal Triads of the individual soul and God's Universal Tree. This divine inheritance is the sheer gift of God's goodness and love. In response and inspired by the compassion growing in our heart center, we may express our gratitude and love by humbly serving God's plan: first, by working toward its fulfillment in ourselves in prayer and action; and secondly, more by silent example and emanations than by words, we may serve God's plan by making it known to others who are not yet aware of it, and who, like ourselves, thirst for true love, goodness and fulfillment; and who are eager to listen and follow the Spirit within them. In humbly serving God in others, when opportunities arise, we grow closer to God in ourselves.

In the lights-off mode and spiritual path, the Spirit's work of inner purification, healing and rebirth in Christ goes on in secret, in the unconscious. It goes on and on until, one day, the chain reaction of changes in unconscious personality patterns, imagery, motivation, desires and beliefs reverberates up into consciousness and we begin to discover we're living in the Lord inside us and perceiving God's subtle presence everywhere around us. This grace typically develops by degrees. Sometimes it's there and sometimes it's not. Ultimately, it evolves into a blessed homecoming for the soul where one awakens into an abiding sense of God's indescribable intimate presence, as if awakening from sleep or a distracting dream. A new and wonderful light has appeared in our inner consciousness, close as a whisper, deep as a well.

The new light shows us that we're living in God and God's in us as the humble holy ground of our hidden roots, supporting our life in love's deep embrace. This awesome presence within is overwhelming, yet infinitely tender and intimate. In his Last Supper Discourse, Jesus says, "Abide in me as I abide in you" (John 15:4). Some translations say, "Remain in me as I remain in you." This abiding or remaining in the Lord suggests a mutual intimacy of oneness, communion and union that's the golden fruit of prayer in secret.

We're not really free to abide consciously in the Lord as our center until the obstacles to doing so have been removed. The removal of these obstacles by the divine action is the "reward" Jesus mentions in Matthew 6:6 when he says, "Pray to your Father who is in secret, and your Father who sees in secret will reward you." This secret place in our soul is the intimate unconscious in Yesod, where the personality patterns and afflictive emotions of our false-self system reside. The "reward" of contemplative prayer, in which we fully consent to God's presence and action, is liberation from these patterns. Once this work is done, then we're free to "abide" in Christ—the true self—as our integral center of being.

Jesus' instruction to "abide in me" is the way of contemplative prayer and living that comes with receiving the "reward" of inner transformation he alludes to in Matthew 6:6. As we receive this initial "reward" of spiritual inheritance, the next step is to live or abide in the reward. "Abide in me" is an advanced formula for contemplative prayer and life characteristic of the soul's awakening to its true self in Tiphareth in the smaller Tree of Tiphareth in the Spiritual/Moral Triad. The inner way of abiding in Christ is where the process of rebirth in Christ, which began in Malkuth and the Personality/Astral Triad, matures into a new dimension of consciousness opening in the soul. It's the restructuring of consciousness Jesus refers to allegorically as "being born of water and the Spirit" in his dialogue with Nicodemus (John 3:5). Having come into the restructuring of consciousness brought about by the divine action through Centering Prayer, the next stage in our contemplative evolution is learning, with God's kind, patient help, to fully abide in it. Thus we *become* the reward.

In lights-off mysticism, we don't see the work of inner transformation while it's going on, but we do see its results when they bloom up into consciousness and we find our self living in God and God living in us. This stage of spiritual awakening in Tiphareth or Christ is the true goal of both lights-off and lights-on mysticism. It's a gift of grace that comes to us according to our openness and capacity to receive it. Lights-on experiences come and go, but living in the inner awareness of God's presence gradually becomes a continual abiding in communion and union with Christ in daily-life consciousness. This inner rebirth in Christ develops by degrees, perhaps beginning in the Tiphareth of Netzach as our heart turns increasingly toward longing for God in prayer and action. This gift gradually stabilizes and matures in Tiphareth in the small Tree within Tiphareth and evolves further from there.

In 2 Corinthians 5:17, Paul writes, "So whoever is in Christ is a new creation: the old things have passed away; behold, new things have come!" This passage is clearly about inner transformation, the re-creation of our personality expression and consciousness in Christ. The New Jerusalem translation says, "A new being is there to be seen." This new being is the true self of our soul that is reborn in Christ and "abides" or "remains" in the Lord. "Abide in me as I abide in you" is Jesus' teaching for entering into and remaining a new creation in Christ. We may know this new creation for what it actually is only by discovering and experiencing it firsthand in our soul.

The inner process of abiding in Christ is a gift of grace that begins by being experienced intermittently in Tiphareth, in the smaller Trees of Malkuth, Yesod, Hod and Netzach. In moving from contemplation, where one usually first experiences inner abiding, into action, slowing down inside and taking a break from the ego's distracting preoccupations may help us open to the Lord's inner presence in daily life. This is a very delicate and subtle matter involving the balance between inner and outer awareness. By pausing, relaxing and focusing into our self in the immediate moment, we may find a chink in the consciousness-filter of our habitual preconceptions and emotional patterns. Such an opening is a portal to the inner depths of our being in the midst of outer activity.

It's important to note, however, that like Centering Prayer, the process of inner abiding really works by God's grace in us and not by our efforts. It's a sheer gift that comes to us on God's terms and as God wills, not as we will. As Thomas Keating has said, God's presence gradually "insinuates itself" into our consciousness. This, I believe, is the consciousness-restructuring process that leads to abiding more or less permanently in the Lord's presence.

Tiphareth in all the smaller Trees helps us enter and learn the way of abiding in our true center, the heart chakra—which corresponds to the Sphere of Tiphareth in the center of the Tree. This is the center of our true self and the divine indwelling, the Source of our soul's immortal substance. Abiding consciously in our true self is the freedom way where we may live in the peace and preciousness of the present moment in both prayer and action. While in the consciousness of God's inner presence, we feel whole and complete in our self. This is not a state of manic ego-inflation, energy dissipation or pride, but a quiet mood of humility, gratitude and caring for the sanctity of God's creation and everyone in it. This inner attitude brings us into Tiphareth in the small Tree of the Sephira Tiphareth, our true center of being.

In this state of abiding in Christ, we are content to be whoever we are or appear to be, with our roles in life and so forth, while inwardly we're living a resurrected life in the peace and preciousness of God's presence. Outer recognition loses importance when we have the inner recognition of Christ's presence abiding in us. There's enough, more than enough to overflow the soul's cup with inner joy and fulfillment in the wealth of heart's treasure. Our entire outlook and approach to life are changed by the secret inner rebirth and awakening to life in Christ. We inhabit the stability of inner abiding with Christ in the motionless moment's center of now—around which time and events turn like a revolving stage of actions and relationships moving through our consciousness as we too move and play our part.

The way of abiding is an apophatic openness that drops preconceptions, sees the ego as factual fiction (not our true identity) and lives with simple humility and faith in God's hidden presence in the immediate now-moment. It does this in both prayer and action. Our focus shifts from the outer to the inner, from what passes to what abides. The integration of these two (outer and inner) in the one Christ is the way of abiding. It is a gift of God's grace that unites contemplation and action, Martha and Mary (Luke 10:38–42) in the soul.[5] Abiding in Tiphareth, our soul's true center, is the foundation of a blessed sanity, the inner rock of our continuing salvation and rebirth in Christ.

VIII

Thomas Keating has said that the awakening of the true self, which begins our rebirth in Christ, is not the end of our spiritual journey but the beginning of true Christian life. It's the beginning of the real Christian life because now we're at last free to live the Christian life without interference from the false self. The gift of abiding in Christ, if we welcome and accept it, begins our mature Christian life on the spiritual level.

Inner abiding in Christ is a contemplative gift, meaning it's something the Lord brings about in us with our consent and cooperation. We may think of it as a further extension or fruit of Centering Prayer, where the sincerity and depth of our humility, faith and consent correlate to the openness and depth of our receptive capacity. Our love and longing for God play key roles in this dynamic process of interrelationship with Christ.

On the Tree of Life, overcoming the false self and shifting our center of identity into the true self correlates to the restructuring of our consciousness in spiritual ground and abiding in Christ more or less permanently. Awareness of God's subtle inner presence is built into this restructuring of consciousness, which takes place in the holy Sphere of Tiphareth in the Spiritual/Moral Triad. This renewal and reorientation of our conscious center is far more valuable than any number of temporary lights-on experiences, which come and go. It's the inner rebirth and transition that brings our human life into our spiritual life, and our spiritual life into our human life. In Qabalah, this is symbolized by the interlaced triangles in the Star of David, the human patriarch of Jesus. In Hebrew, "David" means "Beloved" and Jesus Christ, born in "the House of the Beloved," is the most beloved Son of God the Father. The birth of Christ in our soul under the Star of David is the union of our human nature with our divine nature in the center of the Tree.

Though we must, of necessity, describe and discuss Malkuth and the Spheres of the Personality/Astral Triad separately, together with the smaller Trees within them, in actuality we live, grow and function in all of them simultaneously all the time. This is reflected in their interrelationships and in the fact that different individuals may evolve to different levels within the smaller Trees of all the Sephiroth. Reaching the level of Tiphareth in the smaller Tree of each Sphere is the point of integration, liberation and rebirth in Christ within that Sphere. Daath/the Cloud, into which non-conceptual Centering Prayer takes us, is the passage place of transition in each Sphere's smaller Tree into its Supernal Triad and thence into the Malkuth of the smaller Tree in the next higher Sphere. This continues on up the Tree in reverse numerical order of the Sephiroth (10 to 1). Once the level of Tiphareth or rebirth in Christ is reached in the smaller Trees of Malkuth and the Spheres of the Personality/Astral Triad, the soul may permanently transition into rebirth in Christ (Tiphareth) in the Spiritual/Moral Triad. This is a great homecoming for the soul, but not the end of its journey—as mentioned above.

Centering Prayer opens up a new pathway to God in the soul. The smaller Trees within the Sephiroth show us that there are many degrees or grades of consciously contacting Tiphareth, the heart center, and the other Spheres on the Tree of Life. The restructuring of consciousness that takes place in big Tiphareth marks the transition to permanently abiding consciously in God through our rebirth in Christ.

In the meantime, experiences of God's subtle presence may come up at any time as feelings of peace, joy, wellbeing, compassion, etc. Such little epiphanies are indications of the Spirit's presence and movement in the soul. We're always in God's presence and consciousness, as is all of created reality, and we'll do well in our spiritual journey to cultivate the humble habit of consciously abiding in God's presence at all times, whether we feel it or not. Inner abiding in Christ and allowing the inspiration, love and guidance of this true center in Tiphareth to inform and permeate all we do is the essence of Christian spiritual life.

In Hod of the smaller Tree in Tiphareth, the mind grasps the vision of Christ in the heart of all souls, loving righteousness and longing to redeem us. In Netzach of the smaller Tree in Tiphareth, the soul awakens to the full passion of love's emotional longing for union with God in Christ. This is the deepest meaning of every lover's longing for the beloved. When the soul attains, by God's loving grace, to Tiphareth in the smaller Tree of Tiphareth, its Personality/Astral Triad, abiding fully in Christ, is raised up into the Spiritual/Moral Triad. Lover and beloved, Christ and our soul, are then united on the spiritual level. This is our homecoming, where we discover, in all truth, God's love and longing for us are infinitely greater than our love and longing for God.

EPILOGUE

As the personality structure is deconstructed and reconstructed again and again in moving through Daath/the Cloud and up the small Trees within the Personality/Astral Triad and beyond, it becomes more and more a true expression of the divine image in the soul. This process of consciousness evolution together with our growth in love marks the ascending stages of our rebirth in Christ on the Tree of Life.

In this book, we've described the Tree of Life as a whole and outlined our spiritual journey on the Tree through its human stages in Malkuth and the Personality/Astral Triad up into the beginning of its divine stages in Tiphareth and the Spiritual/Moral Triad. These are the stages of spiritual growth and consciousness evolution that should be of most practical relevance and interest to readers of this book. Anyone who has advanced into the permanent consciousness of the divine indwelling in Tiphareth and beyond would have little, if any, need for the information in these pages.

As a map of spiritual growth and rebirth in Christ through Centering Prayer, this book has charted in general outline nearly the first half of the soul's journey of return up the Tree of Life. There are, of course, many more details and much more to be discovered and said. Further insights may be intuited about our continuing rebirth in Christ by reflecting on the implications of our spiritual inheritance and the Spheres of the Spiritual/Moral and Supernal Triads as described in the first part of the book.

NOTES

Introduction

1. See "The Origins of Centering Prayer" in Thomas Keating, *Intimacy with God*.

2. See/hear the video "Prayer in Secret," session 1 of "Six Follow-up Sessions to the Introductory Workshop to Centering Prayer." Also, see the introduction in Thomas Keating, *Open Mind, Open Heart* (all references are to the 20th-anniversary edition).

3. See Thomas Keating's books *Open Mind, Open Heart*; *The Mystery of Christ*; *Invitation to Love*; *Intimacy with God*; and *The Human Condition*; also parts 2, 3 and 4 of "The Spiritual Journey" video series by Fr. Keating.

4. Human consciousness is capable of focusing on only a limited range of experience in any given moment. As what we focus attention on becomes magnified in consciousness, other things we could be focusing on drop away into subconsciousness or the unconscious. Hence, the vital function of memory which allows us to retrieve some—but not all—information and experiences from subconsciousness and the unconscious. It's fairly common knowledge that we use only a small percentage of our brain's capacity. In its current stage of evolution, our physical-brain consciousness possesses limited capacities of awareness and functioning. It is possible, however, for consciousness to go beyond the brain into nonphysical realms of reality and experience, e.g., in sleep, dreams, out-of-body experiences, deep prayer and meditation.

5. See "Apophatic/Kataphatic Contemplation" in the glossary and introduction of *Open Mind, Open Heart*, p. 5.

6. In *Open Mind, Open Heart*, Keating writes, "To emphasize the experiential knowledge of God, the Greek Bible used the word *gnosis* to translate the Hebrew *da'ath*, a much stronger term that implies an intimate kind of knowledge involving the whole person, not just the mind" (p. 140).

1. Meeting the Tree

1. The B.O.T.A. is the "Builders of the Adytum." This religious organization is a Temple of Christian Qabalah founded by Dr. Paul Foster Case (1884–1954) in the early decades of the Twentieth Century. *Adytum* is Greek for Inner Shrine or Temple. B.O.T.A. offers a series of correspondence courses authored by Dr. Case and his successor, Rev. Dr. Ann Davies. These teachings and the inspiration to develop B.O.T.A. were received intuitively by Dr.

Case, and later by Rev. Davies, from an "inner voice" of spiritual guidance and wisdom in true Qabalistic fashion, since "Qabalah" means, among other things, "the received" or "revealed teaching."

2. See Bernard Brandon Scott, *Hear Then the Parable: A Commentary on the Parables of Jesus*, Fortress Press, 1989.

3. Teresa of Avila's map is presented in her classic work, *The Interior Castle*. John of the Cross' inner map is elaborated in his great works, *The Ascent of Mount Carmel* and *Dark Night of the Soul*. Thomas Keating's integrative map of the spiritual journey combines traditional Christian spirituality with modern insights from psychology, sociology, anthropology, comparative religions and the sciences. This original, comprehensive map may be found in his books *Open Mind, Open Heart*; *The Mystery of Christ*; *Invitation to Love*; and *Intimacy with God*, as well as on his "Spiritual Journey" video series and "The Psychology of Centering Prayer" video.

4. See, for example, Anne and Daniel Meurois-Givaudan, *The Way of the Essenes: Christ's Hidden Life Remembered,* and Barbara Thiering, *Jesus and the Riddle of the Dead Sea Scrolls.*

3. THE SUPERNAL TRIAD.

1. My sources include the published written and recorded teachings of Rev. Ann Davies of the B.O.T.A., books by Dr. Paul Foster Case, Dion Fortune, *Mystical Qabalah* and unpublished papers by Diane Frey. The inspirational ideas in Diane's manuscript have been essential for me to write about the Tree of Life as a map of spiritual growth.

5. THE PERSONALITY/ASTRAL TRIAD

1. There is, on the Tree of Life, the invisible Sephira, Daath/the Cloud, that corresponds to the Great Abyss separating the universal consciousness of the Supernal Triad from the individual consciousness of the Spiritual/Moral Triad and World of Formation. Dion Fortune, in *The Mystical Qabalah*, locates Daath on the Middle Pillar in the World of Creation where the energy path connecting Chokmah and Binah intersects the Middle Pillar. In Ms. Fortune's model of the Tree, the three Sephiroth of the World of Creation carry the attributes of Knowledge (Daath), Understanding (Binah) and Wisdom (Chokmah), the three contemplative gifts of the Spirit.

The B.O.T.A. teachings locate Daath on the Middle Pillar between the World of Formation and the World of Creation, below the Supernal Triad. Daath/the Cloud is called "invisible" because it cannot be conceived by the intellect. It is utterly apophatic (without images) and corresponds to nonconceptual prayer or pure contemplation, which is the practical means for crossing the Great Abyss.

I'm inclined to agree with the B.O.T.A. idea regarding the position-
ing of Daath on the Tree, since once we're in the Supernal Triad, we've
already crossed the Great Abyss. However, since Daath is transcendent and
non-conceptual, and since locating it on the Tree is a conceptual exercise,
perhaps any controversy about this is ludicrous?

2. See Jung's works *The Archetypes and the Collective Unconscious* and *Aion*,
where Jung identifies the figure of "the Christ" as the most appropriate
representation of psychic wholeness for the Western psyche.

3. A classic example of this is early-twentieth-century Russian psychologist
Ivan Pavlov's dog, which was conditioned to automatically salivate at the
ringing of a bell after having been given meat to eat immediately following
the ringing of a bell several times. The bell would ring and the dog would
salivate when no meat was present.

6. Malkuth/Kingdom and Daath/the Cloud

1. In his book, *The Biology of Belief*, cell biologist Bruce Lipton explains in
detail and offers empirical scientific evidence to support the vital connection between body, mind and the new biological science of "epigenetics,"
which shows us that cells possess consciousness and respond to both
chemical and non-chemical, i.e., neural, stimuli. These neural stimuli
include thoughts, images and emotions.

2. Paul Foster Case, writing in *The True and Invisible Rosicrucian Order*,
says that the *Qlippoth* or "Shells" are destructive forces that are best left
alone.

3. See/hear Bruce Lipton's *Biology of Belief* and "The Wisdom of Your Cells."

4. In his recorded *Heartfulness: Transformation in Christ* series (with Betty
Sue Flowers), Thomas Keating speaks of "the purification and development
of the unconscious into Cosmic Consciousness" (CD or DVD no. 3, seg-
ment 9, "Divine Transformation").

5. *Open Mind, Open Heart: 20th Anniversary Edition*, p. 12.

6. See/hear Fr. Meninger's video series, *The Cloud of Unknowing*, set 5,
Christian Contemplative Heritage, "Our Apophatic Tradition," from Contemplative Outreach, 1994.

7. Our Divine Inheritance

1. This information is based on lecture set 3 of the "Sunday Service Messages"
by Rev. Ann Davies of the B.O.T.A. These talks include "The Qabalistic
"Study of Creation" (Gen. 1)"; "Qabalistic Truth about Adam and Eve"
(Gen. 2); and "Understanding Good and Evil through Qabalah" (Gen. 3).
The allegorical sense of scripture is that in which the characters, events
and messages in the Bible are internalized and interpreted as pertaining to
different energies, voices and parts of the self within the individual soul.

The other senses of scripture are the literal (where it's taken at face value), the moral (which teaches about right and wrong) and the spiritual (the non-conceptual, contemplative dimension). The allegorical sense of scripture may also be considered as the symbolic or mythic dimension of scripture concerning the events of our inner spiritual life.

2.   The movement of created reality's energy and images down the Tree of Life is reflected in the Qabalistic interpretation of the first four chapters in the Book of Genesis. According to this interpretation, Genesis One takes place in the Supernal Triad, which contains the Archetypal World (Kether) and the World of Creation (Chokmah and Binah). Genesis Two and Three are said to occur in the World of Formation (Spiritual/Moral and Personality/Astral Triads). And Genesis Four, which marks the birth of individual souls into human incarnation, is said to occur in the World of Manifestation (Malkuth).

By placing the biblical account of creation on the Tree of Life, some of its apparent contradictions, e.g., between Genesis 1 and 2 as two seemingly different accounts of the creation, may be resolved, since they occur on different levels or in different Worlds on the Tree. Also, different and sometimes conflicting ways of interpreting scripture in general may be understood or resolved by relating them to the different perspectives and levels of consciousness associated with the different Sephiroth, Triads and Worlds on the Tree, which represents the multidimensional reality of God's creation (the visible and invisible worlds), and the individual soul.

8. Unconscious Personality Patterns

1.   See Thomas Keating, *The Mystery of Christ*; *Invitation to Love*; and *Intimacy with God*; also, "The Spiritual Journey" video series, talks 6–17.

2.   *Human Ground, Spiritual Ground: Paradise Lost and Found* reflects on Thomas Keating's conceptual background for Centering Prayer.

3.   For details of happiness programs, see *Human Ground, Spiritual Ground*.

9. Personality Patterns on the Tree of Life

1.   See COEX Systems in Stanislav Grof's *Realms of the Human Unconscious*; *Beyond the Brain*; and *Psychology of the Future*.

2.   *Addiction and Grace*, p. 14.

3.   The astral body or etheric double is said to continue functioning consciously for some time following physical death. There are differing views of nonphysical subtle bodies expressed in the traditional and contemporary metaphysical, esoteric and energy-medicine literature. See Cyndi Dale, *The Subtle Body: An Encyclopedia of Your Energetic Anatomy*; Caroline Myss, *Anatomy of the Spirit: The Seven Stages of Power and Healing*; Torkom Saraydarian, *Other Worlds*; Edward Reaugh Smith, *The Burning Bush*;

Alice A. Bailey, *A Treatise On White Magic*; and Manly P. Hall, *The Secret Teachings of All Ages*.

4. See "complex(es)" in Carl Jung's Collected Works, vol. 8, *The Structure and Dynamics of the Psyche*. An autonomous complex is a configuration of motivation, energy and desire in the soul that takes on a life of its own, usually in the unconscious (Yesod), apart from the conscious intentions of the personality.

5. See Thomas Keating, *The Mystery of Christ*, part 2, "The Easter Ascension Mystery."

6. Habits are described as magnetic whirls of vibratory patterns in the Builders of the Adytum CD series, "The Qabalistic Power of Words" by Rev. Ann Davies.

10. THE INNER WORK OF CENTERING PRAYER

1. The Welcoming Prayer, *Lectio Divina* and use of an active prayer sentence are practices taught by Contemplative Outreach in the forty-day praxis Booklets of the Contemplative Life Program and may be accessed via their website at www.contemplativeoutreach.org. See also the praxis on forgiveness, the appendices in *Open Mind, Open Heart* and Cynthia Bourgeault, *Centering Prayer and Inner Awakening*.

2. I learned this formula for keeping one's inner peace intact many years ago from Swami Amar Jyoti of Poona, India, at a spiritual retreat in the Rocky Mountains. One of this teacher's aphorisms was, "You become what you oppose," and is perhaps similar to Jesus' words in Matthew 5:39, "Do not resist an evil doer." Then, Jesus goes further by saying, "But if anyone strikes you on the right cheek, turn the other also; and if anyone wants to sue you and take your coat, give your cloak as well." In confounding the "eye for an eye and a tooth for a tooth" logic of common sense human justice (Matt. 5:38), Jesus invokes a higher spiritual law based on universal love and oneness. This higher, unitive law originates in spiritual ground and transcends the duality of opposites that is the basis of our thinking in human ground.

3. Jesus whipping the money changers and overturning their tables in the Temple of Jerusalem (John 2:14–16) is a striking example of this.

4. See Thomas Keating, *The Fruits and Gifts of the Spirit*.

5. St. John of the Cross writes about the Nights of Sense and Spirit in his classic work, *The Dark Night of the Soul*. Also see Gerald May's book of the same title and Thomas Keating, *Invitation to Love* and *Spiritual Journey* videos, no. 18, *The Night of Sense*, and no. 19, *The Night of Spirit*.

6. See, for example, Thomas Keating, *Open Mind, Open Heart*; *Invitation to Love*; *The Mystery of Christ*; and *Intimacy with God*; and *The Spiritual Journey* video and audio series; plus the video *The Psychological Experience of Centering Prayer*.

7. For some practical guidelines on forgiveness, see William A. Meninger, *The Process of Forgiveness;* Contemplative Outreach's forty-day Contemplative Life Program praxis, *Forgiveness: Growth in Love;* and Fr. Carl J. Arico, *Forgiveness: Growth in Love,* and the CD *The Forgiveness Prayer Practice.*

11. THE MYSTERY OF DAATH/THE CLOUD

1. The seven spinal chakras of Eastern yoga are located on the Tree's Middle Pillar, which balances the energies of the side Pillars: Severity and Mercy. The four Sephiroth actually on the Middle Pillar are: 1) Malkuth, the root chakra at the base of the spine; 2) Yesod, the sacral/reproductive center below the belly; 3) Tiphareth, the heart chakra; and 4) Kether, the crown chakra. The point of intersection on the Middle Pillar with the energy path connecting Hod and Netzach is the solar plexus chakra; the throat chakra is located where the energy path between Geburah and Chesed crosses the Middle Pillar; and the third-eye chakra is located where the energy path between Binah and Chokmah meets the Middle Pillar.

According to Dr. Paul Foster Case in his book, *The True and Invisible Rosicrucian Order,* the inner holy planets and associated metals are: 1) Saturn, lead—root chakra; 2) Mars, iron—sacral/reproductive chakra; 3) Jupiter, tin—solar plexus; 4) Sun, gold—heart chakra; 5) Venus, copper— throat chakra; 6) Moon, silver—third-eye; and 7) Mercury, quicksilver— crown chakra. In Qabalah, there is also an angel associated with each of the chakras or inner holy planets, e.g., the Archangel Michael is associated with the Sun, gold and the heart chakra. This demonstrates that the Western mystical tradition of Qabalah and the Tree of Life has its own ancient system of kataphatic meditation and spiritual development comparable to the inner yoga practices of the ancient East as found, for example, in Hinduism and Buddhism. The Secret Wisdom of Israel involving Qabalah and the Tree has been called "the yoga of the West."

A comprehensive cross-cultural reference book on the soul's energy centers, as conceived of in various traditions is Cyndi Dale, *The Subtle Body: An Encyclopedia of Your Energetic Anatomy.* Though mainstream Christianity has nothing to say on the topic of the chakras or subtle energy centers, illustrations of "the sacred heart of Jesus" clearly represent the perfected heart center of divine love, and the nimbus or halo around the heads of saints and holy people in many Christian drawings and paintings corresponds to a highly developed third-eye and crown chakra. In *Kundalini Energy and Christian Spirituality,* Philip St. Romain shares his spontaneous personal experiences of lights-on mysticism in the context of Christian prayer practice. For deepening silence in Centering Prayer, see David Frenette, *The Path of Centering Prayer.*

2. I first heard the phrase, "All methods end in silence," many years ago from Swami Amar Jyoti, a guru from India, who was comparing a variety of spiritual practices leading to *Samadhi* or enlightenment.

3. As mentioned earlier, the Four Qabalistic Worlds are the Archetypal World corresponding to Kether; the World of Creation corresponding to Chokmah and Binah; the World of Formation corresponding to the

Spiritual/Moral and Personality/Astral Triads; and the World of Manifestation corresponding to Malkuth. Assigning a complete Tree of Life to each of the Four Worlds adds further dimensions of detail and possibility to the Tree as representing the complex divine image, the macrocosmic totality of created reality and the full potentiality of each individual soul. The pattern of the Tree is like a holon pattern that reproduces itself again and again throughout the physical and metaphysical dimensions of created reality and evolving consciousness within the unifying divine consciousness of non-created Reality.

4. See *The Collected Works of John of the Cross;* Gerald May, *Dark Night of the Soul;* and Keating, *Spiritual Journey* series, video talks 18 and 19.

5. See Lex Hixon, *Mother of the Buddhas: Meditations on the Prajnaparamita Sutra.*

6. See *Tao Te Ching* (tr. Ch'U Ta-Kao); *Lao Tzu: Tao Te Ching* (ed. Richard Wilhelm); and *The Wisdom of Laotse* (ed. Lin Yutang).

7. See Lu K'yuan Yu, *The Secrets of Chinese Meditation* (Charles Luk), and *The Secret of the Golden Flower,* translated and explained by Richard Wilhelm, with a foreword and commentary by C. G. Jung that illumines the differences and similarities between Eastern Meditation and Western Depth Psychology.

8. See Lex Hixon, *Great Swan: Meetings with Ramakrishna,* and Swami Amar Jyoti, *Dawning: Eternal Wisdom, Heritage for Today.*

9. Many of this teacher's extraordinary experiences as a spiritual seeker are recounted in the fictional story by Swami Amar Jyoti, *Spirit of Himalaya.*

12. REBIRTH IN CHRIST

1. Thomas Keating stresses this point in talk no. 19 of his *Spiritual Journey* series, "The Night of Spirit."

2. See Andre Louf, OCSO, *The Way of Humility* (tr. L. S. Cunningham).

3. See Keating, *Fruits and Gifts of the Spirit,* for an enlightening discussion of these inner spiritual treasures.

4. Similarly, Tiphareth in Hod concerns our intellect and how it interacts with our emotions. There's a two-way exchange of energies between Netzach and Hod along the horizontal energy path connecting them. Likewise, there are energy paths connecting Hod and Netzach to Yesod at the bottom of the Personality/Astral Triad. In this way, the Spheres of the Personality/Astral Triad all interact and influence one another by exchanging energies. This occurs among the larger Spheres and also in the smaller Trees within them, the mini-Sephiroth of which are connected to their corresponding larger Spheres. From this we may intuit the diverse complexity of relationships among all ten Sephiroth on the Tree of Life.

5. See Thomas Keating's wonderful book, *The Better Part.*

References

Anonymous. *The Cloud of Unknowing* (tr. C. A. Butcher). Boston: Shambhala, 2009.

———. *The Cloud of Unknowing: And The Book of Privy Counseling* (ed. W. Johnston). New York: Doubleday, 1973.

———. *Meditations on the Tarot,* (tr. R. Powell). New York: Tarcher, 2002.

———. *The Secret of the Golden Flower: A Chinese Book of Life* (tr. R. Wilhelm). London, Routledge & Kegan Paul, 1967.

Bailey, A. A. *A Treatise on White Magic.* New York: Lucis Publishing, 1969.

Bourgeault, C. *Centering Prayer and Inner Awakening.* Cambridge, MA: Cowley, 2004.

Case, P. F. *The Tarot: A Key to the Wisdom of the Ages.* Los Angeles: Builders of the Adytum, 1990.

———. *The True and Invisible Rosicrucian Order.* York Beach, ME: Samuel Weiser, 1985.

Contemplative Life Program. *Active Prayer.* Butler, NJ: Contemplative Outreach, 2005.

———. *Forgiveness.* Butler, NJ: Contemplative Outreach, 2005.

———. *Welcoming Prayer.* Butler, NJ: Contemplative Outreach, 2005.

Dale, C. *The Subtle Body.* Boulder, CO: Sounds True, 2009.

Frenette, D. *The Path of Centering Prayer: Deepening Your Experience of God.* Boulder, CO: Sounds True, 2012.

Frey, D. *Papers on the Tree of Life.* Unpublished, 2009–2012.

Frey, K. *Human Ground, Spiritual Ground: Paradise Lost and Found: A Reflection on Centering Prayer's Conceptual Background.* Great Barrington, MA: Portal Books, 2012.

Fortune, D. *The Mystical Qabalah.* Boston: Weiser, 2000.

Grof, S. *Beyond the Brain: Birth, Death, and Transendence in Psychotherapy.* Albany: SUNY, 1985.

———. *Psychology of the Future: Lessons from Modern Consciousness Research.* Albany: SUNY, 2000.

———. *Realms of the Human Unconscious: Observations from LSD Research.* New York: Dutton, 1976.

Hall, M. P. *The Secret Teachings of All Ages: An Encyclopedic Outline of Masonic, Hermetic, Qabballistic and Rosicrucian Symbolical Philosophy.* Los Angeles: Philosophical Research Society, 1988.

Hixon, L. *Great Swan: Meetings with Ramakrishna.* Boston: Shambhala, 1992.

———. *Mother of the Buddhas: Meditations on the Prajnaparamita Sutra.* Wheaton, IL: Quest, 1993.

Holy Bible: New Revised Standard Version. New York: Oxford University, 1989.

John of the Cross, Saint. *The Collected Works of St. John of the Cross* (tr. K. Kavanaugh and O. Rodriguez). Washington, DC: ICS, 1979.

Jung, C. G. *The Collected Works of C. G. Jung.* Princeton, NJ: Bollingen Series XX, Princeton Univ. Press:

———. *Aion: Researches into the Phenomenology of the Self,* vol. 9, part 2, 1979.

———. *The Archetypes and the Collective Unconscious,* vol. 9, part 1, 1980.

———. *The Structure and Dynamics of the Psyche,* vol. 8, 1969.

Jyoti, S. A. *Dawning.* Boulder, CO: Truth Consciousness, 1991.

———. *Spirit of Himalaya.* Boulder, CO: Truth Consciousness, 1988.

Keating, T. *The Better Part.* New York: Continuum, 2000.

———. *Fruits and Gifts of the Spirit.* New York: Lantern Books, 2000.

———. *The Human Condition.* New York: Paulist, 1999.

———. *Intimacy With God.* New York: Crossroad, 1994.

———. *Invitation to Love.* New York: Continuum, 1992.

———. *The Mystery of Christ.* New York: Continuum, 2003.

———. *Open Mind, Open Heart: 20th Anniversary Edition.* New York: Continuum, 2006.

K'uan Yu, L. *The Secrets of Chinese Meditation.* York Beach, Maine: Samuel Weiser, 1969.

Lao Tzu. *Tao Te Ching* (tr. Ch'u Ta-Kao). New York: Samuel Weiser, 1973.

———. *Tao Te Ching* (tr. R. Wilhelm). New York: Arkana, 1986.

———. *The Wisdom of Laotse* (ed. L. Yutang). New York: Random House, 1948.

Lipton, B. H. *The Biology of Belief: Unleashing the Power of Consciousness, Matter, and Miracles.* Carlsbad, CA: Hay House, 2008.

Louf, A. *The Way of Humility* (tr. L. Cunningham). Kalamazoo, MI: Cistercian Publications, 2007.

May, G. *Addiction and Grace: Love and Spirituality in the Healing of Addictions.* San Francisco: Harper, 1991.

———. *Dark Night of the Soul: A Psychiatrist Explores the Connection between Darkness and Spiritual Growth.* San Francisco: Harper, 2004.

McTaggart, L. *The Field: The Quest for the Secret Force of the Universe.* New York: HarperCollins, 2002.

Meninger, W. A. *The Loving Search for God: Contemplative Prayer and the Cloud of Unknowing.* New York: Continuum, 1994.

———. *The Process of Forgiveness.* New York: Continuum, 1996.

Meurois-Givaudan, A. and D. Meurois-Givaudan. *The Way of the Essenes: Christ's Hidden Life Remembered*. Rochester, VT: Destiny Books, 1993.

Myss, C. *Anatomy of the Spirit: The Seven Stages of Power and Healing*. New York: Three Rivers, 1996.

New American Bible. New York: Catholic Publishing, 1991.

The New Jerusalem Bible. New York: Doubleday, 1985.

St. Romain, P. *Kundalini Energy and Christian Spirituality: A Pathway to Growth and Healing*. New York: Crossroad, 1991.

Saraydarian, T. *Other Worlds*. West Hills, CA: T.S.G. Publishing, 1990.

Scott, B. B. *Hear Then the Parable: Commentary on the Parables of Jesus*. Minneapolis: Fortress, 1990.

Smith, E. R. *The Burning Bush*. Great Barrington, MA: Anthroposophic Press, 1997.

Teresa of Avila. *The Interior Castle* (tr. K. Kavanaugh and O. Rodriguez). Mahwah, N.J.: Paulist Press, 1979.

Thiering, B. *Jesus and the Riddle of the Dead Sea Scrolls: Unlocking the Secrets of His Life Story*. San Francisco: Harper, 1992.

OTHER REFERENCES

Audio:

Rev. Ann Davies: Lectures on Genesis 1-3 as understood in Qabalah, Lecture Set Three; "The Qabalistic Power of Words;" "Tree of Life" and "Tarot" CD Series. Available from Builders of the Adytum; ph. 323-255-7141 or www.bota.org.

Bruce H. Lipton, Ph.D.: "The Wisdom of Your Cells: How Beliefs Control Your Biology." Available through Sounds True; ph. 1-800-333-9185 or www.soundstrue.com.

Video:

Thomas Keating: "The Spiritual Journey Series;" "Prayer in Secret" from Six Follow-up Sessions to the Introductory Workshop on Centering Prayer; "The Psychological Experience of Centering Prayer," from The Method of Centering Prayer, Set I of the Christian Contemplative Heritage: "Our Apophatic Tradition" Series; "Heartfulness: Transformation in Christ," with Betty Sue Flowers. Available through: Book Store at www.contemplativeoutreach.org or ph. 1-800-608-0096.

William A. Meninger: "The Cloud of Unknowing," Set V from: The Christian Contemplative Heritage Series. Available through: Book Store at www.contempativeoutreach.org or ph. 1-800-608-0096.

CONTEMPLATIVE OUTREACH is a spiritual network of individuals and small faith communities committed to living the contemplative dimension of the Gospel. The common desire for Divine transformation, primarily expressed through a commitment to a daily Centering Prayer practice, unites our international, interdenominational community.

Today, Contemplative Outreach annually serves over 40,000 people; supports over 120 active contemplative chapters in 39 countries; supports over 800 prayer groups; teaches over 15,000 people the practice of Centering Prayer and other contemplative practices through locally-hosted workshops; and provides training and resources to local chapters and volunteers. We also publish and distribute the wisdom teachings of Fr. Thomas Keating and other resources that support the contemplative life.

Contemplative Outreach, Ltd.
10 Park Place, 2nd Floor, Suite B
Butler, New Jersey 07405

973-838-3384
Fax 973-492-5795
Email: office@coutreach.org
www.contemplativeoutreach.org

KESS FREY was born in 1945 and grew up in the Eagle Rock neighborhood of North Los Angeles. In 1968, he graduated in Psychology at the University of California, Irvine. He has studied Eastern and Western philosophy, psychology, and religion since 1965, with particular interests in meditation and depth psychology. He was raised Catholic and is a Catholic Christian who honors the contemplative dimension of all religions and spiritual paths. His principal spiritual teachers have been Lama Anagarika Govinda (German), Chogyam Trungpa, Rinpoche (Tibetan), Swami Amar Jyoti (East Indian), and, since 1989, Fr. Thomas Keating (American).

Mr. Frey has lived in Anchorage, Alaska since 1983, where he worked with school-age children for twenty years. He has been involved with Centering Prayer since 1989, is affiliated with Contemplative Outreach, Ltd., and offers introductory Centering Prayer workshops, facilitates prayer groups and silent retreats, and is active in prison ministry. He is the author of three previous books: *Satsang Notes of Swami Amar Jyoti* (1977), *The Creation of Reality* (1986), and most recently, *Human Ground, Spiritual Ground: Paradise Lost and Found: A Reflection on Centering Prayer's Conceptual Background* (2012).